GLOBAL RECESSION - CAUSES, IMPACTS AND REMEDIES

SHADOW BANKING AND ITS ROLE IN THE FINANCIAL CRISIS

GLOBAL RECESSION - CAUSES, IMPACTS AND REMEDIES

Additional books in this series can be found on Nova's website under the Series tab.

Additional e-books in this series can be found on Nova's website under the e-book tab.

FINANCIAL INSTITUTIONS AND SERVICES

Additional books in this series can be found on Nova's website under the Series tab.

Additional e-books in this series can be found on Nova's website under the e-book tab.

GLOBAL RECESSION - CAUSES, IMPACTS AND REMEDIES

SHADOW BANKING AND ITS ROLE IN THE FINANCIAL CRISIS

DEVIN A. JENKINS
AND
MARLIN I. COLLINS
EDITORS

nova publishers
New York

For permission to use material from this book please contact us:
Telephone 631-231-7269; Fax 631-231-8175
Web Site: http://www.novapublishers.com

NOTICE TO THE READER

Library of Congress Cataloging-in-Publication Data

ISBN: 978-1-62081-703-2

Published by Nova Science Publishers, Inc. † New York

CONTENTS

PREFACE

Shadow banking refers to bank-like financial activities that are conducted outside the traditional commercial banking system, many of which are unregulated or lightly regulated. Many of the activities performed within the shadow banking system take funds from savers and investors and ultimately provide them to borrowers. Within this broad definition are investment banks, finance companies, money market funds, hedge funds, special purpose entities, and other vehicles that aggregate and hold financial assets. These entities are critical players in the markets for securitized products, structured products, commercial paper, asset-backed commercial paper, repurchase agreements, and derivatives. The activities of these firms financed substantial economic activity, albeit indirectly. This book examines the nature and scope of the shadowing banking system and its role in the financial crisis.

Chapter 1- Shadow banking refers to bank-like financial activities that are conducted outside the traditional commercial banking system, many of which are unregulated or lightly regulated. Many of the activities performed within the shadow banking system take funds from savers and investors and ultimately provide them to borrowers.

Within this broad definition are investment banks, finance companies, money market funds, hedge funds, special purpose entities, and other vehicles that aggregate and hold financial assets. These entities are critical players in the markets for securitized products, structured products, commercial paper, asset-backed commercial paper, repurchase agreements, and derivatives. And the activities of these firms financed substantial economic activity, albeit indirectly.

At their peaks in 2007 and 2008, shadow banking-related markets financed substantial economic activity. The U.S. repurchase agreements (repo) market was over $4.5 trillion at its peak, asset-backed commercial paper

(ABCP) was roughly $1.2 trillion, financial commercial paper (CP) was roughly $800 billion, nonfinancial CP was roughly $220 billion, and securities lending was roughly $600 billion. For reference, commercial banks' deposits were $7.3 trillion at the end of 2008. Shadow banking entities also existed outside the United States. Those linked to major European banks played an important role in the crisis.

Chapter 2- Nearly eight decades ago, after a series of banking crises led to the Great Depression, the United States put in place broad protections over the financial system. These reforms – deposit insurance, prudential rules to limit risk-taking by banks, and improved transparency and investor protection in our securities markets – alongside the Federal Reserve's role as lender of last resort, laid the foundation for a more stable banking industry for several decades.

Over time, however, the financial system outgrew those protections. A large parallel financial system emerged outside of the framework of protections established for traditional banks. A great diversity of financial institutions emerged to provide banking services to individuals and companies, and they were allowed to operate without being subject to the same constraints applied to traditional banks. The shift in mortgage lending away from banks, the growth of the relative importance of non bank financial institutions, the increase in the size of investment banks, and the emergence of a range of specialized financing vehicles are all manifestations of this phenomenon.

Chapter 3- Henry M. Paulson, served as Secretary of the Treasury during the recent financial crisis. Mr. Paulson is proud of the work we in government did to save our nation's financial system from collapse and chaos, and our economy from disaster. Even so, the crisis caused human suffering that simply cannot be measured. The American people deserve—and policymakers will benefit from—an understanding of the broad and diverse causes of the crisis. The job of providing that explanation falls to this Commission, and it is an awesome responsibility.

Many mistakes were made by all market participants, including financial institutions, investors, regulators, and the rating agencies, as well as by policy makers. Most of these are well understood, and, importantly, policymakers are currently addressing some major regulatory structure and authority issues that either allowed the pre-2007 excesses in our system or made it difficult to address the crisis. Nonetheless a number of the root causes are not being addressed and remain sources of danger to our country.

The author starts by giving his views on the fundamental causes of the financial crisis, and then turn to the specific topic of today's hearing—the so-called “shadow banking” system. His views are based on his long experience in the financial markets, the author’s time as Secretary of the Treasury during the financial crisis, and the consideration he has given to these issues in the year-and-a-half since he left government.

Chapter 4- Paul McCulley is a managing director and portfolio manager with PIMCO.

Mr. McCulley’s comments today will try to offer a framework for understanding the nature of the “shadow banking system,” and linking it to the core functions performed by the conventional banking system. I will conclude with some thoughts on lessons learned from the financial crisis.

Before turning to this topic, the author provides a brief overview and background of PIMCO and his role with the firm. PIMCO is an investment management firm founded in 1971, based in Newport Beach, California. PIMCO employs approximately 1,300 people, some 900 of whom work in our two U.S. offices. They also have 9 offices outside of the U.S. PIMCO manages retirement and investment assets for more than 8 million people in the U.S. and millions more around the world. Their clients include pension funds that represent public sector employees at the state and local level, unions, universities, foundations, endowments and private companies that employ Americans from all walks of life.

Chapter 5- Broadly speaking, threats to financial stability can arise in two ways: first, through the rapid deterioration or failure of a large institution with leverage sufficient to have widespread knock-on effects and, second, through the breakdown of a significant market in which large numbers of leveraged actors depend upon similar sources of liquidity and, importantly, backup liquidity in periods of stress. These two sources of systemic risk can be, and usually are, related. In fact, the severity of the recent crisis might be explained as an explosive combination of the two. But the different origins of risk call for different or, perhaps more precisely, complementary, policy responses.

To date, reform in financial regulation and supervision has focused mainly on large regulated institutions: Three examples are the just-announced Basel III capital rules, much of the Dodd-Frank Act, and the Federal Reserve’s revamping of its large holding company supervision. Of course, attention has also been paid to the second source of systemic risk, notably in Dodd Frank’s provisions for prudential supervision of payments, clearing, and settlement systems. But more will need to be done in this area, particularly as new constraints applicable to large regulated institutions push more activity into the unregulated sector.

In: Shadow Banking and Its Role ... ISBN: 978-1- 62081-703-2
Editors: D. A. Jenkins and M. I. Collins

Chapter 1

SHADOW BANKING AND THE FINANCIAL CRISIS*

Financial Crisis Inquiry Commission

INTRODUCTION

The purpose of this preliminary staff report is to describe the nature and scope of the *shadow banking system*. Section II offers a definition of shadow banking and an overview of its role in the crisis. Section III describes the composition, characteristics, and evolution of the shadow banking system. Section IV explains why the key episodes of the financial crisis have been described as bank-like "runs" on shadow banking markets and discusses the vulnerabilities that the crisis revealed in these markets.

I. EXECUTIVE SUMMARY

Shadow banking refers to bank-like financial activities that are conducted outside the traditional commercial banking system, many of which are unregulated or lightly regulated. Many of the activities performed within the shadow banking system take funds from savers and investors and ultimately provide them to borrowers.

* This is an edited, reformatted and augmented version of a Preliminary Staff Report of the Financial Crisis Inquiry Commission, dated May 4, 2010.

Within this broad definition are investment banks, finance companies, money market funds, hedge funds, special purpose entities, and other vehicles that aggregate and hold financial assets. These entities are critical players in the markets for securitized products, structured products, commercial paper, asset-backed commercial paper, repurchase agreements, and derivatives.[1] And the activities of these firms financed substantial economic activity, albeit indirectly.

At their peaks in 2007 and 2008, shadow banking-related markets financed substantial economic activity. The U.S. repurchase agreements (repo) market was over $4.5 trillion at its peak, asset-backed commercial paper (ABCP) was roughly $1.2 trillion, financial commercial paper (CP) was roughly $800 billion, nonfinancial CP was roughly $220 billion, and securities lending was roughly $600 billion. For reference, commercial banks' deposits were $7.3 trillion at the end of 2008.[2] Shadow banking entities also existed outside the United States. Those linked to major European banks played an important role in the crisis.

The shadow banking system was extremely vulnerable to financial stress in three ways: (1) some institutions were highly leveraged; (2) they relied disproportionately on short-term funding markets; and (3) they did not benefit from explicit government support prior to the crisis. As a result, the shadow banking system was vulnerable to panics, just as traditional banks were in the years before deposit insurance. In the panics of 2007 and 2008, many investors withdrew funds from shadow banking system entities, even entities that may potentially have been solvent. Investors knew that such entities could not survive a run, and no investor wanted to be among the last to withdraw. Withdrawals of funding forced entities to sell assets at depressed prices to raise cash, which had the potential to further harm firms' solvency.

This vulnerability of shadow banking entities spilled over to commercial banks. When the shadow banking entities came under pressure, major U.S. and European commercial banks were called upon to provide funds to these entities under agreements that were triggered by disruptions in the market. Thus, the commercial banks came under funding pressures themselves. Even commercial banks that had not provided these backstop agreements reduced the amount they were willing to lend in interbank or other money markets. Knowing the markets were disrupted, commercial banks began to hoard funding in case they themselves began to have trouble raising funds in wholesale markets.

These dynamics played out in three distinct episodes: (1) the liquidity crisis in the summer of 2007; (2) the failure of various liquidity markets and the run on Bear Stearns in the winter of 2008; and (3) the panic of September 2008. During each episode, as in 1930s-era depositor runs on commercial banks, investors, in large numbers, demanded their money back from various shadow banking markets and instruments. The shadow banking system suffered a debilitating loss of confidence as assets were written down and liquidity evaporated: as creditors began to doubt the solvency of an entity, they withdrew funds, prompting deleveraging and asset sales into illiquid markets, further depressing market prices, and eroding the equity of firms holding related assets.

In each of these episodes, the government stepped in to provide unprecedented funding and guarantees. In the latter part of the crisis, this aid was extended to institutions and investors that had no prior claim on taxpayer support. Critically, the Federal Reserve established a series of funding facilities that were directly aimed at improving investor confidence and liquidity in the shadow banking system. With each of these extraordinary measures, the Federal Reserve effectively extended to the shadow banking system its role as the lender of last resort, a role that the central bank had traditionally reserved for commercial banks and savings institutions. Such support was essential to restarting financing in many non- financial sectors that depended indirectly on the shadow banking system.

Shadow Bank Instruments

Money market funds: mutual funds that invest in short-term, low risk instruments such as government securities, commercial paper, certificates of deposit, repurchase agreements, and discount notes.
Hedge funds: unregistered investment companies that serve high net-worth or institutional investors and may pursue complex strategies and investments.
Investment banks: institutions that assist in the issuance of securities, operate as brokers and dealers for various instruments, and trade for their own accounts.
Finance companies: institutions that primarily extend credit to businesses and consumers but do not take deposits.
Asset-backed commercial paper (ABCP) conduits and structured investment vehicles (SIVs): Legal entities that hold assets and use those assets as collateral to issue debt either in the form of ABCP (ABCP conduits) or in the form of ABCP and other notes (SIVs).
Government-sponsored enterprises (GSEs): government-chartered institutions, including Fannie Mae and Freddie Mac, that guarantee the timely payment of principal and interest from a pool of mortgages
Other financial guarantors: institutions that guarantee municipal bonds and other securities.

Shadow Banking Institutions and Entities

Unsecured commercial paper and asset-backed commercial paper (ABCP): debt securities that mature in 270 days or less; they are a major source of funding in the U.S. and abroad.
Repurchase agreements (or **repos**): an agreement whereby a market participant holding an asset sells that asset to another party and commits to repurchase the asset at a later date at an agreed-upon higher price. This transaction is economically equivalent to a loan collateralized by the asset.
Securities lending: transactions in which a party lends securities in order to raise cash for investment.
Auction rate securities: long-term bonds with floating interest rates that reset by auctions at regular intervals.
Derivatives: contracts whose pricing is based on a reference product, index, or other security. Some examples are interest rate swaps, exchange rate swaps, total return swaps, and credit default swaps.

II. Shadow Banking

Shadow banking refers to bank-like financial activities that are conducted outside the traditional commercial banking system, many of which are unregulated or lightly regulated. Many of the activities performed within the shadow banking system take funds from savers and investors and ultimately provide them to borrowers.

Within this broad definition are investment banks, finance companies, money market funds, some hedge funds, special purpose entities, and other vehicles that aggregate and hold financial assets. These entities are critical players in the markets for securitized products, structured products, commercial paper, asset-backed commercial paper, repurchase agreements, and derivatives.

The development of the shadow banking system coincided with the proliferation of financial investment options available to households and corporations. Rather than store their savings predominantly in their local commercial bank, thrift, or credit union, households and corporations increasingly invested in mutual funds or kept their savings in pension funds and retirement programs which in turn invested outside of commercial banks. Figure 1 below depicts the increasing share of financial sector assets held outside of traditional depository institutions.

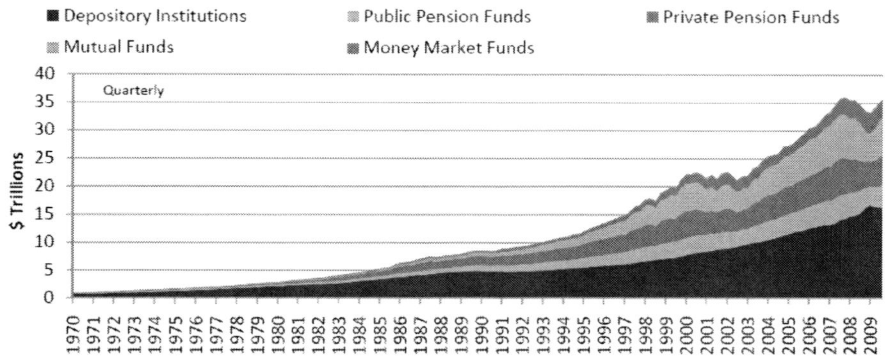

Source: Federal Reserve Board Flow of Funds release.

Figure 1. Assets of Selected Financial Sector Industries.

These assets funded mortgages, other consumer loans, and commercial activities – the same activities funded by the banking sector – through a variety of instruments. At its peak in 2008, the U.S. repurchase agreements (repo) market was over $4.5 trillion,[3] asset-backed commercial paper (ABCP) was roughly $1.2 trillion, financial commercial paper (CP) was roughly $800 billion, nonfinancial CP was roughly $220 billion, and securities lending was roughly $600 billion. For reference, commercial banks' deposits were $7.3 trillion at the end of 2008.[4] The over-the-counter (OTC) derivatives market, which will be the subject of future FCIC work, peaked at $684 trillion in *notional value* in June 2008, representing *gross market value* of $20 trillion.[5]

The shadow banking system facilitated securitization of a substantial fraction of consumer and business credit, including mortgages, auto loans, student loans, credit cards and small business loans. Critical to the financial crisis, the shadow banking system funded mortgages through several channels, most importantly: (1) the higher-risk tranches of mortgage-backed securities were purchased largely by hedge funds and special purpose entities such as collateralized debt obligations (CDOs); (2) the higher-risk tranches of CDOs, in turn, were purchased largely by hedge funds and other CDOs, while the lower-risk tranches of CDOs were frequently hedged through credit default swaps with AIG, a large insurance or financial services firm, or with one of the monoline financial guarantors such as MBIA or Ambac; (3) mortgage lenders financed mortgages prior to securitization, in many though not all cases, through asset-backed commercial paper and other short-term lending markets; and, (4) the investment banks that played a lead role in structuring and selling securitized subprime mortgage products financed themselves significantly through repos and other short-term markets.

Total residential mortgage-backed securities (RMBS) outstanding were approximately $6.7 trillion in 2008, including those issued by the government-sponsored enterprises and those issued by other private entities.[6] For comparison, at the end of 2008, total residential mortgage loans on the balance sheets of depository institutions were $3.2 trillion.[7]

In order to understand how institutions in the shadow banking sector operate, this report will first explain the various functions of a banking system and then compare various aspects of the traditional banking sector and the shadow banking sector. The following sections describe in more detail several of the most relevant financial products and institutions within the system.

A. Shadow Banks and Financial Intermediation

The financial sector helps consumers and businesses get the funds necessary to take part in economic activity. Traditionally, commercial banks and savings institutions have accepted deposits from consumers and businesses, which become the banks' liabilities. These deposits can be withdrawn at any time with little or no penalty and, up to statutory limits, are insured by the U.S. government. In return for depositing money with the banks, savers receive interest payments. Putting these deposits to work, banks provide longer-term loans directly to borrowers (see figure 2). This activity, transforming the risk and/or timing of cash flows between savers and borrowers, is called *financial intermediation*. Over the years, as noted in figure 1, a growing fraction of financial intermediation migrated outside of commercial banks, connecting savers and borrowers through other domestic and international markets. The financial institutions and markets involved in this process comprise the shadow banking system.[8] According to Treasury Secretary Timothy Geithner, "At its peak, the shadow banking system financed about $8 trillion in assets... making it almost as large as the real banking system."[9]

An important aspect of financial intermediation is *maturity transformation*, which is the issuance of short-term liabilities, such as deposits, to fund mortgages, auto loans, and other long-term assets. The financial sector performs this role because businesses and consumers need to borrow money over long periods to invest in houses or factories, but prefer at the same time to hold much of their assets in easily accessible cash and near-cash instruments, such as checking accounts or money market funds.

This maturity transformation, from the financial institution's perspective, creates *liquidity risk*, which is the risk that it will not be able to raise cash or liquid assets to meet demand from depositors withdrawing their money or other short-term creditors needing to be paid. Liquidity risk implies the possibility that a financial institution in need of cash may be required to sell, at distressed prices, assets that it had intended to hold to maturity.

Another primary purpose of financial intermediation is the provision of *credit*. In providing credit, both commercial banks and institutions within the shadow banking system accept and manage *credit risk*, or the potential for those funds not to be repaid in full.

Figure 2 summarizes the traditional banking and shadow banking financial intermediation channels. Through this process, short-term savings are transformed into long-term sources of capital that allow individuals, governments, and corporations to engage in economic activity. As described below, commercial banks or their affiliates often participate in shadow banking markets, supplementing their traditional banking business with new sources of revenue while exposing themselves to new types of financial risk. The two systems often overlap as institutions in both systems frequently engage in the same financial transactions.

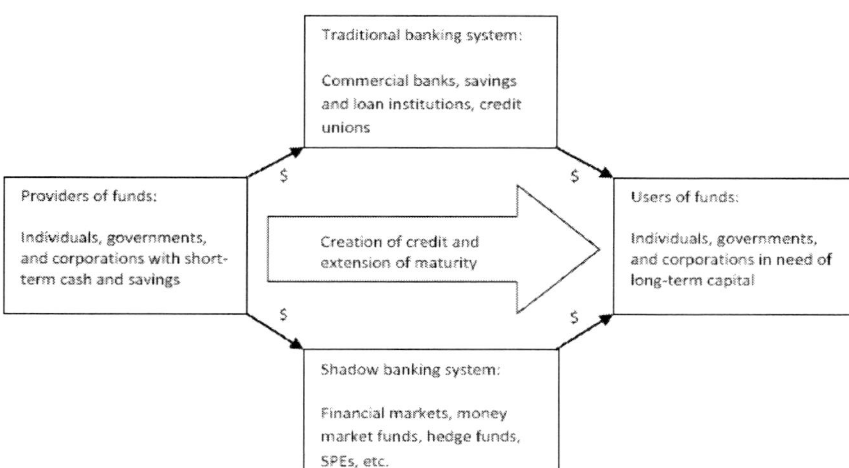

Figure 2. Financial Intermediation through Banks and Markets.

B. Regulation of Shadow Banking

The federal government has regulated commercial banks since the National Currency Act of 1863 because of the important role that banks play in the economy. The introduction of federal deposit insurance in the aftermath of the Great Depression strengthened the case for banking supervision, in part because taxpayers may be at risk when banks fail.

Regulation of nonbanking financial institutions has tended to focus on protecting investors rather than on the safety and soundness of the financial institutions. For that reason, institutions and activities in the shadow banking system were subject to relatively little government regulation. Market participants, meanwhile, proved very adept at creating and offering a variety of financial services in this less regulated sphere.

This regulatory focus on bank safety and soundness promoted the growth of the shadow banking system in three key ways: (1) restrictions on bank activities encouraged nonbanks to develop new services; (2) capital regulations encouraged banks to transfer assets and activities into off-balance sheet vehicles; and, (3) government supervision was less intensive for nonbank financial institutions.

1. Restrictions on Bank Activities

First, and most important, there were stronger restrictions on the activities available to banks and thrifts compared to other types of financial firms capable of offering bank-like products and services. Particularly important were the limitations imposed by the Glass-Steagall Act on commercial banks' investment banking activities.[10]

Investment banks led the rapid growth of market-based forms of borrowing. For example, as discussed below, the commercial paper market became an increasingly popular method of borrowing outside of the traditional banking sector in the 1960s and 1970s. In the 1980s, bank regulators interpreted Glass-Steagall to allow bank holding companies, through their affiliates, to enter this and other markets.

Until 1980, Glass-Steagall also required the Federal Reserve to limit the interest rates that commercial banks could pay savings depositors, creating a market opportunity for money market mutual funds (MMFs).[11] Since returns on investors' shares in MMFs were not subject to the limits on interest rates, their yields exceeded the yields on bank deposits, especially during the high-interest-rate environment of the 1970s. The SEC limited MMFs to investing only in highly rated, short-term, liquid assets; this created a further opportunity for other types of money funds, such as ultra-short bond funds and enhanced cash funds, to offer higher-risk, higher-yield alternatives to eligible investors.

2. Growth of off-Balance Sheet Activities

Second, banks used *credit risk transfer* mechanisms to transfer assets off of their balance sheets. These mechanisms helped firms manage their risks while providing regulatory capital benefits.[12] In many cases, however, banks retained a portion of the credit or liquidity risk of those assets. While regulators required capital to be held against those retained risks, several banks that used these mechanisms experienced large and unexpected losses during the financial crisis, and bank supervisors have since concluded that some capital requirements prior to the crisis were not sufficient.

For example, under the Basel Capital Accord of 1988 (Basel I), banks could reduce their capital requirements by transferring assets into off-balance sheet conduits, which promoted the development of the asset-backed commercial paper market and other special-purpose entities.[13] Banks often provided liquidity support or credit enhancements to these conduits (the structure of the conduits and the support are discussed below). Under U.S. capital rules prior to March 2005, such provisions of support were subject to minimum capital requirements that were lower than they would have been if the assets had been retained on-balance sheet.[14]

Similarly, capital rules effectively promoted the growth of securitization. Under Basel I, as implemented in the U.S., banks could hold less capital on securitized assets relative to the capital required to hold the same dollar amount of underlying assets. Partly in response to that incentive, banks often sold the underlying assets such as mortgages and, in their place, held the higher-rated tranches of mortgage-backed securities. Banks also transferred their credit risk via collateralized debt obligations (CDOs), which segment risk into "tranches" tailored to different types of investors.[15]

3. Varying Forms of Prudential Supervision

Third, where prudential or safety-and-soundness supervision was introduced in the nonbanking financial sector, it was not as intensive as bank supervision.

A series of regulatory and legislative decisions in the 1980s and 1990s, capped by the Gramm-Leach-Bliley Act of 1999 (GLBA), broadened the scope for commercial bank holding companies to participate in securities underwriting and other traditional investment bank activities. By the 2000s, several commercial bank holding companies had significant nonbank subsidiaries. For prudential supervision of these companies, GLBA confirmed the Federal Reserve's role as the "consolidated supervisor" of bank holding companies but required the agency to focus on risks to the regulated and federally insured bank. As a result, activities of supervised bank holding companies outside of the bank, such as some mortgage origination and securities dealing, were not supervised intensively in the 2000s.[16]

In 2004, the SEC created the Consolidated Supervised Entities (CSE) program to supervise investment banks on a consolidated basis.[17] Previously, the SEC supervised only the broker-dealer subsidiaries of investment banks. For example, the SEC supervised Lehman Brothers Inc., the broker-dealer, but not all of Lehman Brothers Holdings Inc, the holding company, which also owned many other subsidiary institutions. Generally, broker-dealers were required to maintain a *net capital ratio* above 2 percent.[18] The net capital ratio, introduced by the SEC in 1975, was intended to ensure that broker-dealers that failed would have sufficient capital to repay customers. For that reason, the calculation of the ratio was more focused on market and liquidity risk than are bank regulatory capital ratios.

Once an investment banking holding company was accepted into the CSE program, its broker-dealer was allowed to use its own internal risk models to compute net capital ratios under the alternative net capital rule, while maintaining a minimum of $1 billion of total equity based on another SEC-defined measure. Falling below $5 billion in total equity would trigger the filing of an early warning notice with the SEC. Upon entry into the CSE program, the holding companies for these broker-dealers agreed to increased reporting to the SEC as well as limits on its activities. According to Appendix E to SEC rule 15c3-1, the SEC could impose additional conditions on the broker or dealer, such as "restricting the broker's or dealer's business on a product-specific, category-specific, or general basis; submitting to the Commission a plan to increase the broker's or dealer's net capital or tentative net capital; filing more frequent reports with the Commission; or modifying the broker's or dealer's internal risk management control procedures. The rule also allows that "if the Commission finds it is necessary or appropriate in the public interest or for the protection of investors, the Commission may impose additional conditions on either the broker-dealer, or the ultimate holding company."

With entry into the CSE program, their holding companies were also required to report risk-based capital. According to standards agreed to by international bank supervisors in the Basel II Capital Accord, 10% is the threshold for a well-capitalized bank.[19] Basel regulatory capital standards are based on ratios of capital to risk-weighted assets rather than to total assets; as a result, required regulatory capital ratios can differ substantially from other commonly used equity-asset ratios. In September 2008, the SEC's Inspector General noted "serious deficiencies" in the CSE program in a report on the SEC's oversight of Bear Stearns:[20] "Bear Stearns was compliant with the CSE program's capital and liquidity requirements; however, its collapse raises questions about the adequacy of those requirements."[21]

Also, investment banks and nonbank financial companies such as AIG, GE Capital, and GMAC were not subject to the same supervisory framework as were bank holding companies. Financial institutions could own depository institutions without being legally designated as bank holding companies, thus avoiding consolidated supervision by the Federal Reserve. They could do this by chartering thrifts (subject to consolidated supervision by the Office of Thrift Supervision) or industrial loan companies (a type of bank, supervised by the Federal Deposit Insurance Corporation, which is not subject to Federal Reserve supervision at the holding company level). The five major investment banks and several other major nonbank financial institutions had ILCs, thrifts, or both, at the time of the financial crisis, which they used to acquire deposits and to access the payment system.

Financial supervisors focused on individual institutions rather than on the stability of the financial system as a whole. The Federal Reserve, as the central bank, has a financial stability mandate as well as a supervisory mandate; in the wake of the crisis, it has committed to better integrating those roles.[22] The President's Working Group on Financial Markets also plays a role in promoting collaboration among supervisors in addressing systemic risks. However, no supervisor was tasked with monitoring systemwide risks that could arise from the combined activities of individual companies – for example, from the financial interconnections among market participants or the over-concentration of risks in a small number of counterparties.

C. The Shadow Banking System's Fragility

As has become clear in hindsight, many shadow banking institutions were extremely vulnerable to financial stress in three ways: (1) they were highly leveraged; (2) they relied disproportionately on short-term funding markets; and (3) they did not benefit from explicit government support prior to the crisis.[23]

1. High Leverage

Financial intermediaries use leverage, that is, they finance themselves largely through debt. Owners (equity or capital investors) face a tradeoff in setting the level of leverage with which they are comfortable. Higher leverage increases profitability for equity investors, as it allows firms to engage in more potentially profitable activities with the same amount of equity invested. However, firms with higher leverage (and thus lower capital) are more likely to become insolvent in the event of significant, unexpected losses. For that reason, governments set leverage limits or capital standards on commercial banks and thrifts in order to increase the size of the equity cushion that is available to absorb losses and to help them survive economic downturns.

However, standards were different for different types of institution. While bank holding companies were leveraged at 10- to 20-to-1 prior to the crisis, leverage for investment banks was 30- to 40-to-1.[24] Meanwhile, the only systematic leverage standards for conduits such as ABCP, described below, were set by credit rating agencies and the due diligence of investors. Special purpose entities created in the securitization process tended to have slim equity tranches, driving their leverage as high as 100 to 1.[25]

When credit losses, particularly on residential mortgage loans, started to exceed expectations in 2007, both banks and shadow banking institutions were subject to losses. This problem first surfaced in thinly capitalized securitizations but quickly spread to vehicles that invested in such securitizations, and then to commercial banks, investment banks, and other market participants that supported these vehicles.

2. Reliance on Short-Term Funding Markets

Commercial banks and thrifts rely heavily on customers' deposits for financing. Deposits from households and businesses are considered *retail* deposits; banks also use *wholesale* deposits, which are large volume deposits, often from other financial institutions. Retail deposits are generally considered "sticky" as customers, with the advent of deposit insurance after the Great Depression, rarely move their deposits from one bank to another. Shadow banks relied almost entirely for their funding on short-term markets such as repos, commercial paper, and securities lenders which behave more like wholesale funding at banks. Bank supervisors tend to view reliance on wholesale funding markets as a risk because such funds are not "sticky" and can be withdrawn quickly.[26]

While short-term funding was appropriate for traditional investment banks to finance their underwriting activities, it became a source of instability as investment banks increased their exposure to long-term, illiquid assets, and the maturity of their liabilities declined to as short as one day. Lacking a core deposit base, investment banks that "borrowed short and lent long" were more vulnerable than commercial banks and thrifts to potential runs.

During a run, creditors withdraw funds or reduce their trading or credit exposure to that entity in an attempt to prevent future losses or delays in payment. If a sufficient number of creditors all demand their funds at once, even if the entity were solvent at the start, the entity may have to sell its assets into a distressed market and recognize significant losses. In this case, the creditors can cause the very default event that they were trying to avoid. Runs can be caused by potentially false rumors about the solvency or stability of an entity. Prior to and during the Great Depression, commercial bank deposit runs occurred frequently. However, since the advent of deposit insurance traditional deposit runs on commercial banks and thrifts have become rare.

3. Lack of Explicit Government Support

Unlike commercial banks and thrifts, the shadow banking system prior to the financial crisis did not have access to explicit government backstop facilities.

Specifically, the government provides two types of programs to the traditional banking system to mitigate liquidity risk – deposit insurance and a lender of last resort – that it has not historically provided to shadow banking institutions.

The lack of these features in the shadow banking system led to substantial fragility.

For banks and savings institutions, deposit insurance mitigates the possibility that many creditors will demand their funds at the same time. At the end of 2007, an estimated 51 percent of deposits at U.S. commercial banks and savings institutions were insured by the FDIC.[27]

Given that their funds are secure, insured depositors have less reason to demand their funds immediately. In contrast, funding in the shadow banking system is not federally insured. Shadow bank funding instruments include unsecured commercial paper, asset-backed commercial paper, repurchase agreements, and medium- and long-term debt. Investment banks used all of these markets for funding.

In the event of an investment bank's bankruptcy, there was a hierarchy among creditors: creditors who loaned via unsecured commercial paper would typically be paid at the same time as other unsubordinated unsecured creditors. Creditors who loaned funds through instruments that operated on a collateralized basis, such as ABCP and repurchase agreements, would cover any potential losses by exercising an explicit first claim on the assets pledged as collateral. Second, the shadow banking system did not have access to the Federal Reserve in its role as the "lender of last resort."

The Federal Reserve uses the Discount Window to provide liquidity by ensuring depository institutions' access to funds, provided that they possess creditworthy assets to pledge as collateral.

Until the Federal Reserve launched the temporary Primary Dealer Credit Facility in March 2008, shadow banks did not have direct access to the Discount Window.[28]

Having a lender of last resort means that even in such a case, the bank can access cash to meet that demand by using its holdings of long-term, safe assets as collateral in return for temporary, short-term funding.

III. Selected Components of the Shadow Banking System

A. Financial Instruments

Markets for several financial instruments grew rapidly in the years prior to the financial crisis. These include commercial paper, repurchase agreements, securities lending, and other lesser-known markets that primarily funded municipal debts. Most of these instruments trade in the *money market*, which is the wholesale market for low-risk, highly liquid, short-term debt.[29]

1. Unsecured Commercial Paper and Asset-Backed Commercial Paper

Commercial paper (CP) is a debt security that matures in 270 days or less and is a major source of funding in the U.S. and abroad. Corporations and other entities can borrow by issuing CP through commercial paper programs. Even though CP is short-term debt, it is usually repaid at maturity with proceeds received from issuing new CP, a process called *rolling CP*. CP is classified into three categories based on the type of entity that issues the security: *corporate*, *financial*, and *asset-backed commercial paper* (ABCP).

Corporate CP and financial CP are *unsecured*, meaning the investor does not have a claim to specific assets of the corporation, but they are not subordinated, which means that CP investors rank ahead of subordinated debt and other more junior investors in the event of bankruptcy. Nonfinancial corporations frequently issue corporate CP to meet immediate demands such as payroll and inventory. Financial corporations frequently issue financial CP to purchase and hold financial assets. Prior to the crisis, unsecured CP and Treasury bills were the largest markets for unsecured debt financing in the U.S. money markets, each totaling about $1 trillion outstanding in 2007.[30]

The third kind of CP, asset-backed commercial paper (ABCP), is collateralized or secured by a claim to specific assets. Typically, a sponsoring firm places assets into a special purpose entity (SPE), and creates a commercial paper program to fund them. This SPE is referred to as an ABCP conduit. Figure 3 depicts the contractual relationships in setting up an ABCP conduit. Investors lend money to the conduit by purchasing the CP. The conduit then uses those funds to buy assets, such as RMBS, from an asset seller, such as the RMBS sponsor.

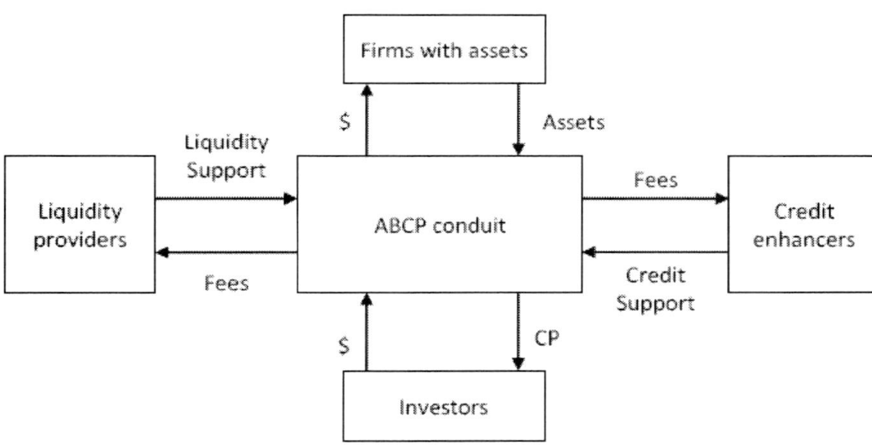

Figure 3. ABCP Conduit Structure.

ABCP investors usually demand some sort of backstop, or assurance, from the parent firm or some other entity such as a financial institution. These backstops can take the form of credit or liquidity enhancements. In the case of credit enhancement, the parent firm or some other entity promises to reimburse ABCP investors for losses arising from changes in the credit quality of the assets in the conduit. Liquidity enhancements are promises to repay ABCP investors if the conduit has trouble rolling its paper due to disruptions in the ABCP markets, provided the collateral maintains its credit quality.

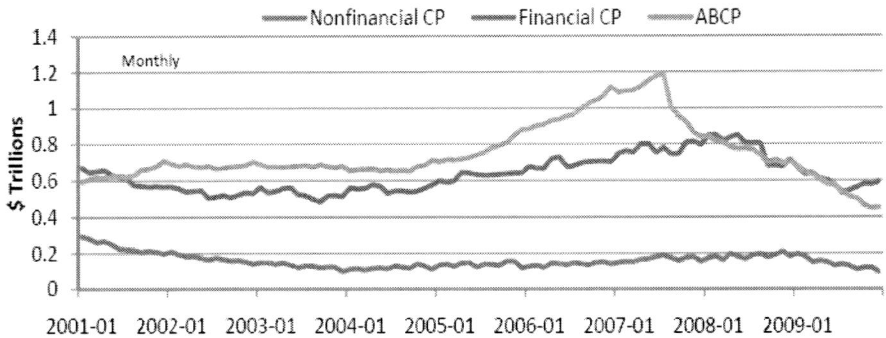

Source: Federal Reserve Board of Governors.

Figure 4. U.S. Commercial Paper Outstandings.

Figure 4 displays the growth of the ABCP market and the financial and nonfinancial CP market from 2001 through 2009. At its peak in 2007, the U.S. ABCP market had about $1.2 trillion outstanding.

Commercial paper is usually rated by the rating agencies. Standard and Poor's uses the ratings A-1+, A-1, A-2, A-3, etc. to rate these short term-instruments with A-1+ being the highest rating. Moody' scale has ratings P-1, P-2, P-3, etc. with P-1 being the strongest rating. Rules for money market funds are based on whether the securities are tier 1 or tier 2: tier-1 securities are those rated "1" by at least two of the rating agencies; a tier-2 security is a security that carries a rating no lower than 2 for the agencies but is not a tier-1 security.[31]

2. Repurchase Agreements

Repurchase agreements (repos) are another important source of short-term funding in the shadow banking system. In a repo transaction, a market participant holding an asset (the seller) sells that asset to another party (the buyer) and commits to repurchase the asset at a later date at an agreed-upon higher price. In this trade, the buyer is essentially making a short-term secured loan to the seller. If the seller fails to repurchase the assets as agreed, the buyer retains the asset (effectively serving as the collateral).

Through the repo market, investors with large asset holdings can lend idle assets to effectively "borrow" cash on a short-term basis. Cash borrowed in this way is collateralized by the securities loaned and this cash can be used for further investment or to pay down debts. Other market participants with large pools of cash, for example money market mutual funds, can "lend" cash in the repo market in order to earn an extra return on their cash positions. The lender of cash earns a fee but also holds (effectively "borrows") the securities that were purchased ("pledged") to secure the borrowed cash. These securities can be further pledged or used as collateral by the securities buyer in activities such as shorting.

It is possible for repurchase agreements to be structured to be accounted for as sales. Otherwise, repurchase agreements will be accounted for as financings or what may be referred to as secured borrowings. The transferor (lender) of securities will reclassify securities held to securities "pledged," record the cash received and the obligation under the repurchase agreement. The transferee recognizes a repurchase agreement asset equal to the amount of cash transferred and reduces cash by an equal amount. The difference between the initial purchase price and the higher repurchase price is effectively interest on a loan. Interest on the cash loaned will be recorded at the time the repo is settled. If the repurchase agreement does not provide for the return of securities that are "substantially the same" as those loaned, the repurchase agreement cannot be recorded as a secured borrowing and will be recorded as a sale.

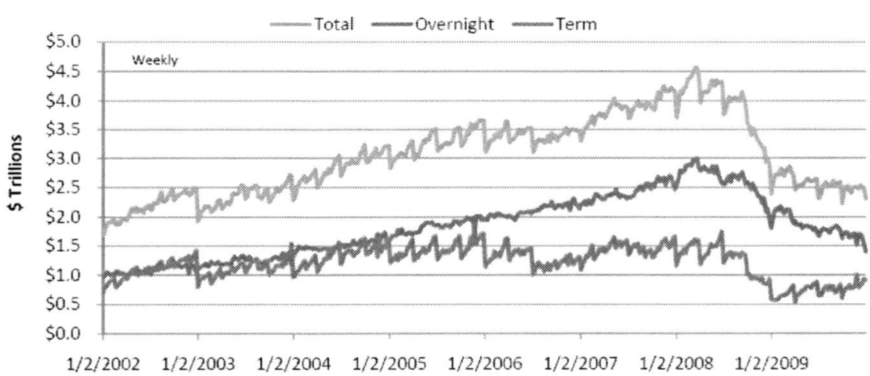

Source: Federal Reserve Bank of New York Survey of Primary Dealers.

Figure 5. Repurchase Agreements Outstanding.

Many forms of securities are used as collateral in the repo market. *Traditional collateral* consists of U.S. Treasuries and agency securities. Agency securities are MBS or discount notes issued by government-sponsored entities such as Fannie Mae and Freddie Mac. Other forms of collateral are referred to as *non-traditional* and can include non-agency MBS, corporate debt, equities, etc. Depending on the type of collateral, the buyer will demand a collateral margin or haircut. For example, for safer forms of collateral, a buyer may ask for $102 in assets for a $100 cash loan. For riskier collateral, the margin or haircut may be larger.

Generally, repo transactions are of a short maturity and fall into one of three categories: *overnight*, *term*, or *open*. Overnight repo refers to transactions with a single-day maturity. Term maturity refers to repos that have a fixed maturity longer than one day. Open maturity repos are deals where both parties have the option to terminate the repo each day.

There are two main settlement methods for repo transactions: *bilateral* and *triparty*. In a bilateral transaction, the seller transfers the assets directly to the buyer and the cash is delivered to the seller. In tri-party repo, both parties to the transaction have cash and collateral accounts at the same third-party clearing bank. The clearing bank verifies that the collateral pledged is sufficient and meets the requirements for the deal, and all parties agree to use collateral values supplied by the clearing bank. JPMorgan Chase and Bank of New York Mellon are the two major tri-party clearing banks for repo transactions.

While estimates of the precise size of the repo market vary, the Federal Reserve Bank of New York does collect data on the positions held by the largest broker-dealers.[32] From a total under $2 billion at the beginning of 2002, broker-dealers' repo financing totaled more than $4.5 trillion outstanding at the peak of the market in 2008. Overnight repo became increasingly prevalent as well. As described below, this market contracted sharply following the collapse of Bear Stearns.

3. Securities Lending

Banks, insurance companies, pension funds, and other financial institutions maintain substantial investment portfolios. At the same time, hedge funds may need securities, for example, to cover short sales. Securities lending refers to the asset lenders (e.g. the pension funds) lending their securities to the securities borrowers (e.g. hedge funds) in return for cash collateral. When the loan is terminated, the securities are returned to the lender and the cash collateral is returned to the borrower.

Securities lending transactions are very similar to repo transactions except that there is no stated maturity, securities are loaned rather than purchased, and the cash is typically reinvested by the securities lender in cash reinvestment pools.

Some financial institutions increasingly lend not only their own securities, but also securities that they hold in custody for customers, with those customers' permission. In those cases, customers share the fee income and any interest or other returns on cash collateral that is reinvested.

4. Auction Rate Securities

Auction Rate Securities (ARS) are long-term bonds that have floating interest rates that reset at regular intervals, usually less than a month.

At each reset date, an auction is held in which holders of the bonds and other interested parties bid on the interest rate they will accept.

The interest rate is set at a rate just high enough that a sufficient number of investors will hold the bonds. However, the holders of the bonds are not required to bid in each auction. With too few bidders, the auction can fail.

In these cases, the investment banks that operate the interest rate auction traditionally would bid and thereby provide support during episodes of illiquidity. However, investment banks typically were not required to bid under the terms of the deal and, in fact, did not during the crisis.

At the end of 2007, total ARS outstanding were about $330 billion. Municipalities were the primary issuers of these bonds, along with other similar instruments.[33]

Using ARS, municipalities financed long-term debt with instruments that investors thought were short-term and relatively risk free. As a result of this maturity mismatch, ARS markets suffered from the same fragilities that were inherent in other parts of the shadow banking system.

And ARS markets also suffered major stresses during the crisis.

5. Derivatives

There is an enormous over-the-counter (OTC) derivatives market and a number of derivatives exchanges in the U.S. and abroad; the derivatives market will be the subject of a future FCIC Preliminary Staff Report.

Over-the-counter (OTC) derivatives commonly used by the financial sector include interest rate swaps, exchange rate swaps, total return swaps, equity swaps, commodity swaps, and credit default swaps (CDS).

These are contracts that trade streams of cash flows referenced to some underlying asset or index in exchange for a fee. For example, a CDS is a credit derivative, a contractual agreement where one party, for a fee, agrees to pay another party if some third party defaults on a liability.

Derivatives were frequently used to facilitate the issuance of ABCP, MBS, and other financial instruments.

For example, monoline financial guarantors such as MBIA and Ambac, which prior to the crisis received the top rating from the credit rating agencies, sold CDS to investors of MBS and collateralized debt obligations (CDOs). Effectively, investors would replace their exposure to the credit risk of these securities with an exposure to the lower perceived credit risk of the monoline guarantor.

As another example, the growing popularity of *synthetic CDOs* created further opportunities for investors to take a bullish or bearish view on mortgage-backed securities.

Synthetic CDOs are similar to traditional CDOs except that the underlying assets are long positions on credit default swaps rather than tangible assets. From 2005 to 2007, subprime MBS-backed CDOs were increasingly synthetic.

B. Institutions and Entities

The shadow banking system consists of various types of institutions that perform financial intermediation through the instruments mentioned above. Figure 6 depicts the relationships among some of the more significant debt instruments and entities involved in financial intermediation. On the left are the liabilities of entities that need to fund short-term expenses, consumer purchases, equipment, real estate, and capital projects. On the right are the assets of entities that have savings to invest. In the middle are several of the entities involved in the financial intermediation process. The colors identify the specific markets and instruments that these entities use. Each institution is portrayed with its assets on the left and its liabilities on the right.

1. Money Market Funds

Money market funds (MMFs) are significant participants in the shadow banking system. Households, businesses and asset managers purchase shares in these mutual funds, which in turn invest those funds in instruments such as government securities, commercial paper (CP), certificates of deposit (CDs), repurchase agreements (repos), discount notes, and other short-term securities. In figure 6, MMFs appear in the middle-right section, providing wholesale funds to money markets through repo, unsecured CP, and ABCP. MMFs are regulated by the SEC and are subject to provisions of the Investment Company Act of 1940. These provisions specify the credit quality, diversification, and maturity of securities that MMFs can purchase.

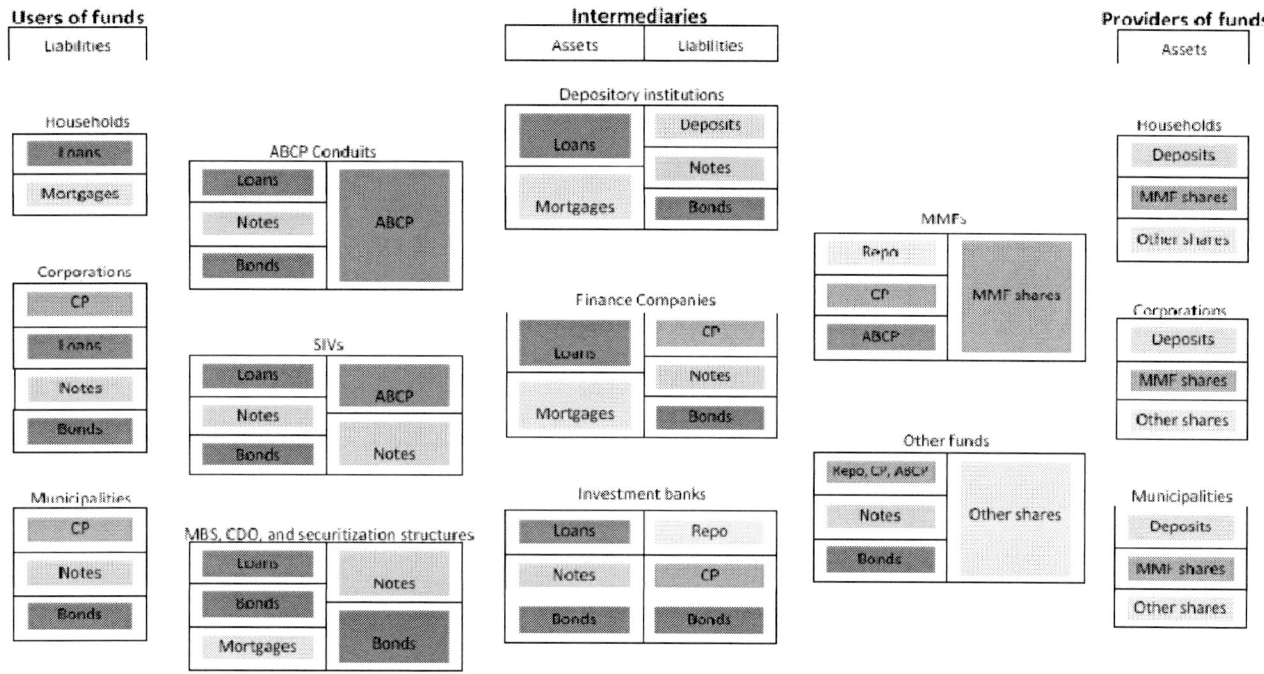

Note. Other funds include securities lending cash reinvestment pools, hedge funds, mutual funds, government investment pools, and other asset managers. CP refers to unsecured commercial paper. Notes are medium-term debt instruments; bonds are long-term debt instruments. Importantly, this figure does not represent all instruments and entities. For example, not included in this diagram are equity securities or securities directly held by households, corporations, and municipalities. Source: Pozsar, 2008.

Figure 6. Selected Financial Intermediation Entities and Debt Instruments.

MMFs are classified based upon the clients they serve and the securities they invest in. Retail MMFs take funds from households and other small investors.In contrast, institutional funds serve corporate investors, pension funds, and other large clients. Government funds invest solely in government issued securities while non-government or prime funds invest also in corporate and other asset-backed instruments.

Table 1. Money Market Fund Family Rankings by Assets as of August 31, 2008

Rank	Family	Assets ($ Mill)	Market Share
1	Fidelity	425,663	12.7
2	JP Morgan	267,921	8.0
3	BlackRock	259,823	7.8
4	Federated	231,117	6.9
5	Dreyfus	199,097	6.0
6	Schwab	194,483	5.8
7	Vanguard	191,478	5.7
8	Goldman Sachs	183,633	5.5
9	Columbia	146,828	4.4
10	Morgan Stanley	112,583	3.4
	Top 10	2,212,626	66.2%
	Total Market	3,342,290	100%

Source: Crane Data.

MMFs can have the look and feel of deposits at commercial banks. Investors may be able to write checks to others using the funds in the MMF, and typically funds may be withdrawn at any time with little or no penalty. However, unlike deposits at commercial banks, MMFs are not guaranteed by the U.S. government. MMFs attempt to maintain a stable $1 net asset value (NAV). Investors depend on the $1 NAV and even the rumor of a fund 'breaking the buck' can spark a run. As a result, if a MMF drops below the $1 NAV threshold, sometimes a parent company will provide support so that investors do not experience losses.

Table 1 shows the largest money market fund families and the amount of assets they managed as of August 31, 2008.

There are a number of other funds that invest in a manner similar to money market funds but are not subject to the same regulatory restrictions. These include cash reinvestment pools managed by securities lenders, sweep accounts, enhanced cash funds, ultra-short bond funds, short-term investment funds, local government investment pools, and offshore money funds.[34] In figure 6, these funds appear in the middle-right section as "other funds."

The major securities lender custodian banks with cash reinvestment pools are JPMorgan, Bank of New York Mellon, State Street, and Northern Trust. Examples of major securities lenders reinvesting their own funds are AIG (prior to the crisis) and state pension funds such as CalPERS.

2. Hedge Funds

Hedge funds are private investment companies that manage funds for high net worth individuals or institutions. Funds invest in various asset classes and use a variety of strategies.[35] In general, hedge funds charge investors a management fee equal to one to two percent of assets under management and a performance fee of up to 20 percent of profits.

By restricting the investor base and not offering their securities to the public, hedge funds are exempt from registration as mutual funds with the SEC under the Investment Company Act of 1940. As a result, precise data regarding the number of hedge funds are not available. It is estimated that as of 2007 there were between 9,000 and 11,000 hedge funds with total assets of over $2 trillion globally, representing 1.5 percent of the total assets under management at pension funds, mutual funds, insurance companies, and banks.[36] However, they represent a much larger fraction of the trading in certain markets such as distressed debt, leveraged loans and some credit derivative markets.[37]

Data from one industry source is shown in figure 7. The tremendous growth in hedge fund assets since 2000 is readily apparent. Following the financial crisis, assets under management fell, but as of 2009 appear to be growing once again. Table 2 shows the ten largest hedge funds as of the end of 2007.

Table 2. Largest Hedge Funds as of December 31, 2007

Rank	Family	Assets ($ Bill)
1	JP Morgan Asset Management	44.7
2	Bridgewater Associates	36.0
3	Farallon Capital Management	36.0
4	Renaissance Technologies Corp.	33.3
5	Och-Ziff Capital Management	33.2
6	D.E. Shaw Group	32.2
7	Goldman Sachs Asset Mgmt	29.2
8	Paulson & Co.	29.0
9	Barclays Global Investors	26.2
10	GLG Partners	23.9

Source: International Financial Services London 2008 Hedge Fund Report.

Note that several of these funds are affiliated with commercial banks, providing one of the links from the shadow banking system to the traditional banking system.

Hedge funds are not generally subject to direct oversight by any federal or state agency. The SEC has the ability to oversee the managers of those funds that are required to register or that voluntarily choose to do so. In 2004, the SEC modified its regulations to require registration by a broader set of hedge fund managers. However, those rules were struck down in a 2006 federal court ruling.[38] As a result, most oversight is done indirectly through the large securities firms regulated by the SEC. The Commodity Futures Trading Commission (CFTC) has access to some information about hedge fund trading on the regulated futures and commodity options markets and also oversees some hedge fund operators which have registered as commodity pool advisers.[39]

Hedge funds utilize the prime brokerage services of broker-dealers. Most hedge funds use the services of more than one prime broker; still, the prime brokerage business is very concentrated. As of year-end 2006, the top three prime brokers, Morgan Stanley, Bear Stearns and Goldman Sachs serviced 58 percent of the hedge fund accounts. The top ten brokers had over 80 percent of the market. This industry structure resulted in brokers being exposed to the hedge fund industry, and concentrated counterparty risk for the hedge funds to the brokers.

Hedge funds are also major trading partners with the large commercial banks and investment banks. For example, many hedge funds borrow cash from these financial institutions in repo transactions with the hedge funds posting their securities as collateral. Also, as already noted, several of the large banks control very substantial hedge funds. Together, these linkages through prime brokerage, as counterparties to broker-dealers, and through ownership, helped spread the crisis throughout the shadow banking system and to the traditional banking sector as well.

3. Investment Banks

Investment banks are firms that assist in the issuance of securities, engage in market-maiking operations, operate brokerages, deal in derivatives, and trade securities for their own accounts. Prior to the crisis some were standalone institutions such as Goldman Sachs and Morgan Stanley, while others operated under large financial holding companies such as Citigroup and JPMorgan Chase.

Investment banks provide liquidity in markets for bonds, equities, derivatives, and repurchase agreements. They provide *prime brokerage* services, allowing hedge funds and asset managers the ability to hold, buy and sell securities. One of the key services is repo financing.

Because investment banks have large holdings of marketable securities that they generally plan to hold only for short periods, they fund a large portion of their balance sheets with repurchase agreements, in addition to unsecured commercial paper and long-term debt, as shown in the lower-middle section of figure 6.

In the 2000s, some investment banks achieved full vertical integration in markets such as mortgage finance, owning mortgage origination and securitization units, off-balance sheet funding vehicles, and mortgage-related asset management units. In this way, investment banks could replace the entire mortgage intermediation process performed by commercial banks. This business also exposed them to more credit risk and duration risk on their balance sheets than they had traditionally been willing to accept.

4. Finance Companies

Finance companies supply credit to businesses and consumers but do not take deposits. Instead, they raise funds by issuing commercial paper and bonds. While they do securitize some of their loans, some finance companies also hold assets on their balance sheets, similar to a traditional bank.

Finance companies appear in the middle of figure 6. There are three main categories of finance companies. Captive finance companies, usually affiliated with automotive or other manufacturing companies, finance dealer inventories or consumer purchases of their products. Commercial finance companies make loans to businesses secured by the assets of the firm or the firm's receivables. Consumer finance companies make loans to consumers for furniture, appliances, and other purchases along with offering credit cards. In the years before the financial crisis, finance companies were also offering mortgages. Total receivables at finance companies at the end of 2006, before the first liquidity episode in the summer of 2007, were approximately $1.9 trillion.

Figure 8 shows the considerable growth of consumer and real estate receivables compared to business receivables at finance companies. Real estate receivables consist primarily of mortgages on one to four family homes. Finance companies also chose to maintain the majority of their receivables on their balance sheets, instead of securitizing them. At their peak, finance companies held about $600 billion of real estate receivables and about $700 billion of consumer receivables on their balance sheets, before trending downward.

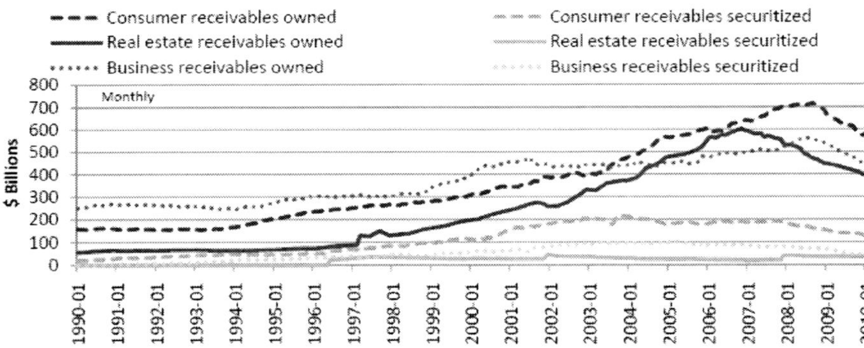

Source: Federal Reserve Board G.20 release.

Figure 8. Receivables Owned or Securitized by Finance Companies.

5. Asset-Backed Commercial Paper Conduits

Developments in securitization and bankruptcy-remote financing allowed the creation of funding vehicles such as ABCP conduits. These funding vehicles sell their own debt and hold assets and securities in trust. They perform credit intermediation and maturity transformation by purchasing diversified assets and funding them in short-term markets.

There are several types of ABCP conduits that can be distinguished by asset holdings, depth of maturity transformation, liability structure, and enhancements. Table 3 displays these types and describes the size and composition of their asset holdings as of June 2007. Multi-seller conduits are the largest category by outstandings and are typically used to fund credit card receivables or trade receivables for corporations that otherwise could not access CP markets.

Other categories of conduits that played a central role in the crisis are the securities arbitrage vehicles and the structured investment vehicles (SIVs). Securties arbitrage vehicles issued ABCP. SIVs issued senior debt in the form of medium-term notes, ABCP, and subordinated securities in the form of capital notes. As shown in figure 6, SIVs (and securities arbitrage vehicles) used those funds to purchase loans, notes, and bonds, including significant amounts of MBS.

Table 3. Global ABCP by program type, June 30, 2007

Program Type	Description	$ billion
Multi-seller Conduits	Diverse asset types	$626
Single-seller Conduits	Single loan types awaiting securitization	$218
Securities Arbitrage	Highly rated securities	$184
Hybrid	Mixed assets	$165
Structured Investment Vehicles (SIVs)	Highly rated securities	$104
Other	CDO-issued paper; others	$95
Total	$1,392	

Source: Moody's.

6. Government-Sponsored Enterprises

Government-sponsored enterprises such as Fannie Mae and Freddie Mac perform two functions associated with shadow banking:[40] guaranteeing timely payment of principal and interest from a pool of mortgage-backed securities (MBS), and purchasing portfolios of bonds funded by then sale of short-term discount notes.

7. Other Financial Guarantors

Other financial guarantors also play a role in shadow banking. These entities, which tend to have high credit ratings, guarantee principal and interest of a bond, a process known as *wrapping*. This is useful to investors because it enhances the credit quality of the underlying bonds. A major subset of financial guarantors called *monolines* arose to wrap municipal bonds.

In the 2000s, monolines such as MBIA and Ambac began wrapping other types of bonds, including mortgage-backed securities (MBS) and collateralized debt obligations (CDOs). These wraps, often in the form of credit default swaps, allowed structured product issuers to issue securities at low interest rates and to receive high ratings from the credit rating agencies. The structured finance guarantee business came to exceed the monolines' traditional municipal business: at the end of 2006, guarantees of asset-backed securities by monoline insurers totaled $2.2 trillion, compared with $1.3 trillion in guarantees of municipal securities.[41]

IV. The Crisis in the Shadow Banking System

The build-up of the financial crisis from early 2007 through the end of 2008 was marked by growing concerns about the financial and economic impacts of falling housing prices, particularly on the subprime mortgage market, a gradual loss of confidence in critical markets and instruments of the shadow banking system, and ultimately a panic that led to the de facto shutdowns of the markets for many shadow banking instruments. This in turn led to fire sales of assets and doubts about the solvency of some entities.

These concerns played out in the shadow banking system in three distinct episodes: (1) the liquidity crisis in the summer of 2007; (2) the failure of various liquidity markets and the run on Bear Stearns in the winter of 2008; and (3) the panic of September 2008. These episodes highlighted the fragility of the shadow banking system. During each episode, as in 1930s-era depositor runs on commercial banks, investors, in large numbers, demanded their money back from various shadow banking markets and instruments. Similar to a run on a commercial bank, the shadow banking system suffered a debilitating loss of confidence as assets were written down and liquidity evaporated. As creditors began to doubt the solvency of an entity, they withdrew funds, prompting deleveraging and asset sales into illiquid markets, further depressing market prices, and eroding the equity of firms holding similar assets even where the assets were not sold.

In each of these episodes, the government stepped in to provide unprecedented funding and guarantees. In the latter part of the crisis, this aid was extended to institutions and investors that had no prior claim on taxpayer support. Critically, the Federal Reserve established a series of funding facilities that were directly aimed at improving liquidity in the shadow banking system during the financial crisis. With each of these extraordinary measures, the Federal Reserve effectively extended to the shadow banking system its role as the lender of last resort, a role that the central bank had traditionally reserved for commercial banks and savings institutions.

A. Episode I: The Liquidity Crisis of 2007

Following the real estate boom, house prices began to fall in 2006 and defaults on subprime mortgages began to rise.[42] These trends continued to worsen throughout 2007 and, starting in early 2007, the credit rating agencies responded by repeatedly downgrading the credit ratings of various tranches of subprime MBS and CDOs.

In the financial markets, the first casualties of these events were subprime mortgage lenders, investment funds that focused on the subprime mortgage market, and ABCP programs with subprime exposure. Concerns spread to hedge funds and commercial paper programs during the summer, and in August global central banks took unprecedented steps to loosen monetary conditions and to provide liquidity to the CP markets.

1. Failure of Mortgage Lenders

The subprime mortgage market was distressed by early 2007. On March 5, HSBC Finance, the largest subprime lender in the U.S., reported that it had set aside $1.4 billion as a provision for subprime credit losses in the fourth quarter of 2006, confirming warnings it had given to investors three months earlier that the decline in house prices had accelerated subprime delinquencies.[43,44]

In a series of March announcements, New Century Financial, the second largest subprime lender, reported an expected financial loss in 2006, citing rising delinquencies, government investigations, and credit pullbacks by lenders. On April 2, the company filed for Chapter 11 bankruptcy protection after cash demands by its warehouse lenders (the banks who had provided financing for subprime mortgage loans awaiting securitization).[45]

By the end of 2007, most independent subprime mortgage lenders that relied on securitization markets for their funding had failed or had been acquired. American Home Mortgage Corp., the 8th largest prime mortgage originator with a $3.3 billion ABCP program, announced it could not fund its obligations on July 31, 2007, and declared bankruptcy on August 6. On August 31, ACC Capital Holdings announced it was closing Ameriquest, the 7th largest subprime originator, and selling its loan servicing unit (and its loan origination platform) to Citigroup.

2. Hedge Fund Losses

In the spring of 2007, two hedge funds run by Bear Stearns Asset Management began to experience rising client redemptions following weakening returns. Both of these funds, the Bear Stearns High-Grade Structured Credit Fund (High-Grade Fund) and the Bear Stearns High-Grade Structured Credit Enhanced Leveraged Fund (Enhanced Leveraged Fund), were heavily invested in subprime assets. On June 7, Bear Stearns announced that it was suspending redemptions from the funds. Creditors refused to continue to provide repo funding and, on June 22, Merrill Lynch seized $800 million in collateral. At the same time, Bear Stearns chose to bail out the High Grade Fund. Nonetheless, both funds declared bankruptcy by the end of July. Losses from subprime assets continued to grow and on August 9, the French bank BNP Paribas announced that it would halt redemptions in three of its investment funds, claiming an inability to value the assets in the funds.

From August 6 to August 8, hedge funds that invested in equities, and specifically those funds using so-called statistical arbitrage strategies, suffered severe losses, even though they appeared isolated from the troubles in the subprime market. These funds were arguably hedged and therefore should not have been vulnerable to market movements. However, market participants have argued that these funds may have been affected when Bear Stearns and other mortgage-focused funds were forced to liquidate their positions rapidly.[46]

3. The Panic and the Run on Commercial Paper

By the summer of 2007, uncertainty in the value of MBS and CDOs began to have more severe effects on the commercial paper market and on the money market, in which financial institutions lend to each other.

In late July 2007, a conduit of the German bank IKB was unable to roll its ABCP due to concerns about the credit quality of its holdings. The bank itself did not support the conduit and a public-private bailout was arranged. The ABCP market immediately came under stress.

As shown in figure 9, spreads on 30-day ABCP immediately widened from near zero to almost 150 basis points in the first part of August 2007.[47] Overall issuance dropped sharply.

Outstanding ABCP fell $190 billion (or 20 percent) in August alone and another $120 billion by year end. New issuance shortened in maturity as well as lenders were unwilling to extend longer-dated credit, as shown in figure 10.

Investors withdrew from ABCP programs in early August, and the withdrawals persisted at those with perceived subprime exposures. Mortgage ABCP programs with assets from just one issuer ("single-seller programs) fell from $35 billion in outstanding commercial paper at the end of May to $4 billion at the end of August.[48] Commercial paper funding for GMAC Financial Services and its subsidiary, Residential Capital Corporation, decreased by $5 billion during this period.[49] Meanwhile, investors fled obligations of structured investment vehicles (SIVs), leading to the fear that SIVs, which held combined assets of roughly $400 billion, would be forced to liquidate their assets at once.[50]

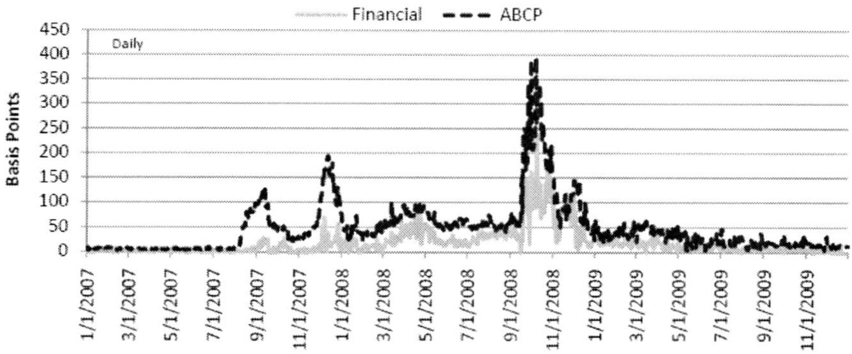

Note. All issuers included in this index have at least one short-term rating of A-1, A-1+, or P-1, with no ratings less than A-1 or P-1.
Source: Federal Reserve Board.

Figure 9. 30-day Highly Rated Commercial Paper Yield Spreads.

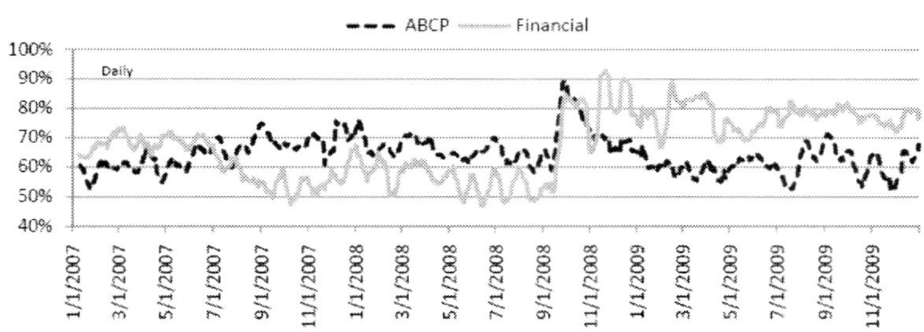

Note. Data points represent 2-week trailing averages of fraction of total issuance maturing in 1 to 4 days by CP type. All issuers included in this index have at least one short-term rating of A-1, A-1+, or P-1, with no ratings less than A-1 or P-1.
Source: Federal Reserve Board.

Figure 10. Fraction of 1-4 Day Issuance for Highly Rated Commercial Paper.

With the markets in turmoil, other ABCP programs also suffered sharp declines. There is evidence that in the earliest phase of the crisis, runs occurred in programs not obviously tied to subprime loans. In particular, *non-mortgage* single-seller ABCP programs shrank from $126 billion at the end of May to $79 billion at the end of August.[51] These funds continued to have trouble raising funds after the initial shock.

As the ABCP market came under stress, interbank lending markets also suffered. Market participants were concerned about the effects on banks from the credit and liquidity support that they had provided to ABCP programs. Interbank lending rates spiked in August 2007 as banks became less willing to lend to each other given the increased uncertainty. Banks built their own cash positions in case they themselves began to have difficulty raising funds in wholesale markets.

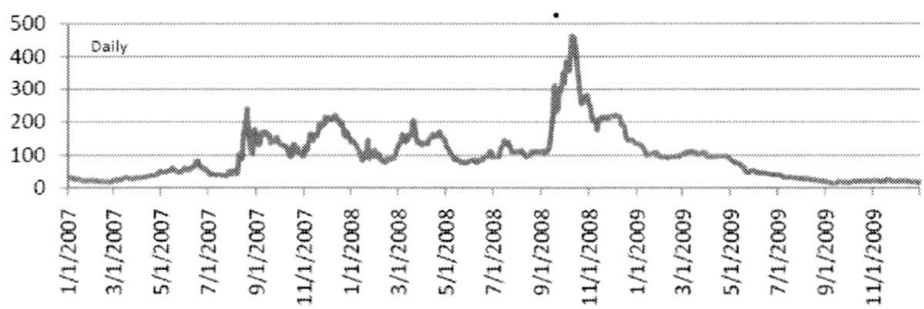

Note. 3-month TED spread is the 3-month LIBOR rate minus the 3-month US Treasury bill rate.
Source: Bloomberg.

Figure 11. 3-Month TED Spread.

Figure 11 shows the TED spread, the difference in the 3-month London Interbank Offered Rate (LIBOR) and the rate on 3-month U.S. Treasury bills. LIBOR is a measure of the rate that banks are willing to lend to each other and therefore reflects a degree of credit risk. In contrast, U.S. Treasury bills are considered risk-free. The difference is therefore, a measure of the perceived uncertainty and credit risk when lending to other banks. Beginning on August 9, 2007, the spreads began to rise. From a historical average of 20 to 60 basis points, the TED spread peaked at 240 basis points later in August. Very quickly, troubles in the shadow banking system spilled over to the traditional banking sector.

4. The Government Response

The panic in the commercial paper markets was met by extraordinary government action. On August 17, the Federal Reserve cut the discount rate by 50 basis points, the first of many cuts aimed at increasing liquidity in the market. Notably, the Board also extended the term of Discount Window lending to 30 days in an effort to offer banking institutions a more stable source of funds.

In response to continued pressures in interbank term lending markets, the Federal Reserve, in December, announced the creation of the Term Auction Facility in December. Under the TAF program, the Federal Reserve auctioned funds to depository institutions for terms of 28 or 84 days. The loans were available to the same depository institutions that were eligible to borrow at the

Discount Window and were fully collateralized with appropriate haircuts. The major advantage of the TAF, according to some analysts, was that it did not carry the same stigma as borrowing from the Discount Window, which in the past had been seen as a sign of weakness.[52] For some TAF loans, the interest rate was below that at the Discount Window.

B. Episode II: Growing Anxiety and the Run on Bear Stearns

Over the course of late 2007 and early 2008, concerns grew about the ultimate cost of the mortgage crisis on the financial sector and banks reported substantial write-downs on mortgages and mortgage-related products. Rating agencies began to raise questions about the ability of financial guarantors to provide contractual protections to structured finance products. In March 2008, these fears concentrated on Bear Stearns, an investment bank which had been a leading participant in originating mortgage-backed securities and which relied heavily on the repo market for its funding.

1. Financial Guarantors

As mortgage default rates increased and asset-backed securities lost value, financial guarantors faced mounting payment obligations. In November and December 2007, the three leading credit rating agencies issued credit outlook warnings or placed on negative watch the top financial ratings of several financial guarantors because of the companies' exposures to CDOs through credit default swaps.[53]

In January 2008, Fitch Ratings downgraded Ambac's insurer financial strength rating from AAA to AA.[54] Moody's placed MBIA's and Ambac's Aaa ratings on review for possible downgrade in January but confirmed both ratings in February and early March after the companies raised $1.6 billion and $1.5 billion in new equity, respectively.[55] S&P downgraded smaller guarantors but similarly affirmed MBIA's and Ambac's AAA ratings after the equity raises.[56]

2. Run on Auction-Rate Securities

The downgrades of monoline guarantors quickly ignited doubts about the credit protection of monoline-wrapped municipal bonds. Bondholders in the auction-rate securities (ARS) market rushed to liquidate their positions. Initially, leading investment banks backstopped the bond auctions, but these actions pressured their balance sheets during a severe liquidity crunch.

Eventually, the investment banks simultaneously stopped bidding, thereby withdrawing liquidity support and causing auction failures. Under the terms for these securities, interest rates reset to much higher contractual limits triggered by auction failures. As a result, issuers were subjected to high short-term interest rates and some investors were unable to exit their positions.[57]

3. Bear Stearns and the Run on Repo and Other Collateral

The collapse of the investment bank Bear Stearns in March 2008 was the next major crisis in the shadow banking system. In early 2008, spreads on agency bonds began to widen again, this time affecting Carlyle Capital, an Amsterdam-listed hedge fund. Further declines in asset prices from the liquidation of part of Carlyle's portfolio, and Bear's direct exposure to Carlyle, made the market nervous about Bear Stearns which itself had substantial exposure to mortgage-related assets. What followed was the rapid elimination of repo funding for the firm.[58] Over a week in March 2008, lenders in the repo markets either refused to roll their positions with Bear Stearns or demanded much more collateral (i.e., increased haircuts) for overnight repo loans. Though secured, investors were not well positioned to hold the collateral in volume, and thus a 'safe' asset market was not immune to panic. Between March 6 and March 13, over $15 billion in funding was pulled from the firm.

At the same time, prime brokerage clients also withdrew their accounts from Bear Stearns. As market rumors spread about the solvency of Bear Stearns in March 2008, over-the-counter (OTC) derivatives counterparties sought collateral calls and *novations* to mitigate potential losses if Bear Stearns fell into bankruptcy.[59] Firms also entered into new derivatives contracts with Bear Stearns constructed in a way to extract cash up front, further hedging bankruptcy risks, which exacerbated the liquidity constraints that Bear Stearns already faced in the marketplace and contributed to its distress.

As a result, Bear Stearns was unable to meet its obligations on March 13. It arranged an emergency bridge loan from the Federal Reserve but after failing to secure additional capital, it was purchased by JP Morgan Chase, with government support, over that weekend.

4. The Falloutfrom Bear and the Government Response

In early March 2008, the Federal Reserve announced the Term Securities Lending Facility (TSLF) and then the Primary Dealer Credit Facility (PDCF).

Under the TSLF, announced just before the sale of Bear Stearns, primary dealers were able to borrow Treasury securities from the Fed by posting eligible securities as collateral; these included federal agency debt, federal agency residential-mortgage-backed securities (MBS), and non-agency AAA/Aaarated private-label residential MBS. They could then use those Treasury securities to obtain cash in the markets. Under the PDCF, broker-dealers could now directly borrow from the Federal Reserve at the primary discount rate. Use of the PDCF reached $40 billion in April 2008 and then declined before spiking to over $150 billion in September. Both of these funding programs were implemented to provide liquidity to the market and to avoid forced sales of mortgage-related assets at depressed prices in order to meet demands from their short-term funders. With these programs now in place, the primary dealers could instead obtain Treasuries or cash – the Fed had stepped in to supply liquidity in the repo market and in essence, open the Discount Window to these non-bank institutions.

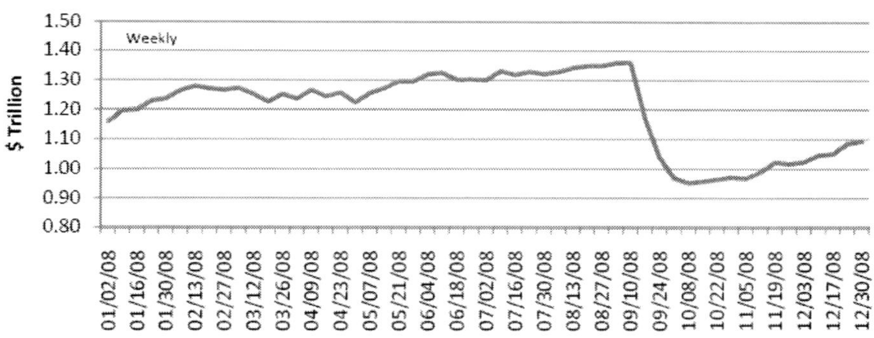

Source: Investment Company Institute.

Figure 12. Total Asssets in Prime Institutional Money Market Funds.

C. Episode III: The Panic of 2008

The year-long liquidity crunch and growing concerns about solvency created the conditions for full-blown panic in September 2008. The collapse of Lehman Brothers in September 2008 was the final trigger that froze the shadow banking system.

1. The Failure of Lehman

Lehman Brothers was under pressure over the course of 2008. From March to September, Lehman was able to raise some capital to aid its liquidity position. It had also sought out potential buyers for the firm. In September, the FHFA placed Fannie Mae and Freddie Mac into conservatorship and extended $200 billion of government support to the institutions. Later that week, Lehman came under pressure similar to Bear Stearns. On September 9, reports emerged that the Korea Development Bank would not purchase Lehman Brothers, contradicting earlier reports, and on September 10 the firm pre-announced $3.9 billion in losses for the third quarter. Repo funding evaporated, prime brokerage clients fled, and increased demands for collateral eventually pushed the firm into bankruptcy.

The failure of Lehman Brothers had repercussions for many components of shadow banking system and the traditional banking system. Most notably, withdrawals increased substantially at money market funds, commercial paper markets came under pressure and certain hedge funds also suffered.

Immediately following Lehman's bankruptcy, one money market mutual fund, the Reserve Primary Fund, realized losses on approximately $785 million of Lehman commercial paper and could not maintain $1 net asset value (it "broke the buck"). In the following week, prime institutional funds experienced net outflows of $300 billion, shown in figure 12, as investors fled possible exposures to other troubled financial institutions. The outflows caused short-term funds to reposition their portfolios, holding cash to brace for redemptions and investing in only the highest quality assets. The pullback severely disrupted liquidity and credit channels.

At the same time, commercial paper spreads, and in particular financial commercial paper, widened even further. As shown in figure 9, ABCP spreads and financial CP spreads rose to 389 and 236 basis points, respectively. Almost all issuance shortened to overnight maturities and many tier-2 issuers were unable to issue paper. As these markets froze, financial firms scrambled for funding and curtailed credit to their borrowers.

Prior to the bankruptcy of Lehman Brothers, prime brokers believed that costs associated with changing brokerages would make their client accounts relatively resilient to concerns about credit quality of the brokerage. When client assets were frozen in Lehman Brothers' London subsidiary, hedge funds transferred cash and securities out of investment banks believed to be under pressure, removing a key source of liquidity and revenue to firms already experiencing pressure from many fronts.

Cash reinvestment pools run by securities lenders also faced pricing and liquidity pressures following the Lehman failure and, as these pools shrank, less funding was available to repo borrowers. International bank supervisors, in a collaborative report on the crisis, noted:

"The severity of the risks associated with securities lending activities—as with prime brokerage—caught many participants by surprise."[60]

Soon after the failure of Lehman, Goldman Sachs and Morgan Stanley applied to become bank holding companies, under Federal Reserve supervision. With the sale of Merrill Lynch to Bank of America several days earlier, this marked the effective end of the investment banking model in the U.S.

2. The Government Response

Following the bankruptcy of Lehman Brothers and the government rescue of AIG, funding markets were in greater turmoil. The Federal Reserve and the Treasury instituted a series of additional measures to counter the runs in the money market funds, to replace the limited funding for short-term unsecured instruments, and to support securitization that had all but ceased. On September 19, the Federal Reserve announced the Money Market Investor Funding Facility (MMIFF) and the Asset-Backed Commercial Paper Money Market Mutual Fund Liquidity Facility (AMLF). Under the AMLF, the Federal Reserve would lend money to depository institutions and bank holding companies to fund the purchase of ABCP from money market mutual funds. At the same time, the U.S. Treasury Department established a temporary guarantee program for the U.S. money market fund industry, effectively insuring the holdings of any publicly offered eligible money market mutual fund – either retail or institutional – that participated in the program. These coordinated actions were meant to calm investor fears, to inject liquidity, and to create a credit backstop akin to deposit insurance for the shadow banking system following the troubles at the Reserve Primary Fund.

The Federal Reserve went even further on October 7, announcing that under the Commercial Paper Funding Facility (CPFF) it would directly purchase ABCP and unsecured CP from issuers. In November the Federal Reserve created the Term Asset-Backed Securities Loan Facility (TALF), a funding facility that would issue loans with a term of up to five years to holders of eligible asset-backed securities (ABS). The TALF was designed to support credit to consumers and business by lending money to issuers of ABS. Eligible collateral initially included highly rated U.S. dollar-denominated ABS backed by student loans, auto loans, credit card loans, and loans guaranteed by the Small Business Administration (SBA). These programs were all instituted to support (or replace) funds for consumer and business purchases and investments that had become unavailable, or very expensive, with the turmoil in the shadow banking system.

D. Credit Market Impacts of the Financial Turmoil

Over the past forty years, the U.S. financial system evolved from a substantially bank-based system to a mixed bank and market based system in which shadow banking system components were the primary sources of funds for several kinds of consumer and business activity. As a result, the runs on shadow banking markets had a major impact on the financial system as credit for consumers and businesses was greatly reduced or hindered. This was clearest in subprime mortgage origination, but other credit markets such as car loans, student loans, municipal finance, commercial real estate and small business finance were all severely constrained in the wake of the crisis.

The decline in these markets was driven by several factors. First, the reduction in demand for asset-backed securities directly led to a decline in the availability of funds for consumer and business credit. The collapse of other markets led to a decline in direct funding for many firms. Facing unprecedented redemptions, money market funds refused to purchase CP, making it difficult for companies to raise cash. A number of tier-2 CP borrowers were hit particularly hard, and some firms are on the record pointing out that they were unable to roll their CP and as a result, were left without cash for needs such as payroll and inventory. The backstops at the commercial banks were further strained given the tumult in the market and the pressures commercial banks faced.

Second, the collapse of the shadow banking system led to the demise of many financial institutions. Many independent mortgage companies and those owned by broker-dealers went bankrupt or ceased operations beginning in late 2006. The closure of such firms led to the evaporation of the organizational capacity to extend this credit as well. Even were the funds available, the commercial banks that had traditionally funded mortgages would not have had the personnel or technology in place, at least in the near term, to replace the closed firms.

Throughout these market convulsions, many financial firms were crippled, and some only survived with substantial government assistance. Their capital was depleted and many of their revenue channels were extinguished or impaired by the decline in financial activity. This condition severely restricted their capacity to provide funding to consumers, businesses, and governments, reinforcing reductions in real economic activity around the world and magnifying the ensuing recession.

REFERENCES

Ashcraft, Adam B., Morten L. Bech, and W. Scott Frame, *The Federal Home Loan Bank System: The Lender of Next-to-Last Resort?*, November 2008.

Barth, James, *The Rise and Fall of the U.S. Mortgage and Credit Markets*, Milken Institute, 2009.

Basel Committee on Banking Supervision, *Basel II: International Convergence of Capital Measurement and Capital Standards: a Revised Framework*, June 2004.

Basel Committee on Banking Supervision, *Consultative document: Strengthening the resilience of the banking sector*, December 2009.

Bernanke, Ben, *Financial Regulation and Supervision after the Crisis: The Role of the Federal Reserve*, October 23, 2009.

Center for Responsible Lending, *Losing Ground: Foreclosures in the Subprime Market and Their Cost to Homeowners*, December 19, 2006.

Covitz, Daniel M., Nellie Liang, and Gustavo A. Suarez, *The Evolution of a Financial Crisis: Panic in the Asset-Backed Commercial Paper Market*, August 2009.

Crescenzi, Anthony and Marcia Stigum, *Stigum's Money Market*, 2007.

Dudley, William, *More Lessons from the Crisis*, November 13, 2009.

Fitch Ratings, *SIV Market Has Disposed of 95% ofAssets Since July 2007*, July 7, 2009.

Gorton, Gary, *Slapped in the Face by the Invisible Hand: Banking and the Panic of2007*, 2009.

Government Accountability Office, *Hedge Funds: Regulators and Market Participants are Taking Steps to Strengthen Market Discipline, but Continued Attention is Needed*, January 2008.

Han, Song and Dan Li, *Liquidity Crisis, Runs, and Securities Design: Lessons from the Collapse of the Auction Rate Securities Market*, June 15, 2009.

Joint Forum, Basel Committee on Banking Supervision, *Credit Risk Transfer*, March 2005.

Joint Forum, Basel Committee on Banking Supervision, *Credit Risk Transfer: developments from 2005 to 2007*, July 2008.

Khandani, Amir and Andrew Lo, *What Happened to the Quants in August 2007?*, November 2007.

Moody's Investor Service, *ABCP Market At A Glance: U.S. ABCP Single-Seller Mortgage Market Snapshot*, August 2007 (Moody's 2007a), September 2007 (Moody's 2007b).

Pozsar, Zoltan, *The Rise and Fall of the Shadow Banking System*, Moody's, July 2008.

Securities and Exchange Commission Office of Inspector General, *SEC's Oversight of Bear Stearns and Related Entities: The Consolidated Supervised Entity Program*, September 2008.

Senior Supervisors Group, *Risk Management Lessons From The Global Banking Crisis Of2008*, October 2009.

GLOSSARY

Asset-Backed Commercial Paper (ABCP): Short-term debt that has a fixed maturity of 270 days or less. The debt is backed by some financial asset, such as trade receivables, consumer debt receivables, or auto and equipment loans or leases. A firm that wants to issue ABCP will place assets in a special purpose entity (SPE) to issue the ABCP. The SPE, which is typically created by a bank or other financial company, is a legally separate entity from the firm.

Auction Rate Securities (ARS): Long-term bonds that have floating interest rates that reset by Dutch auction at regular intervals, usually less than a month.

Bank Holding Company: A company that has control over any bank, or over any company that becomes a bank, as "bank" and "control" are defined in the Bank Holding Company Act of 1956. The Federal Reserve is responsible for supervising bank holding companies even if the bank that the company controls is under the primary supervision of a different federal agency.

Basel Capital Accord of 1988 (Basel I): A set of international banking regulations put forth by the Basel Committee on Banking Supervision, which set out the minimum capital requirements of financial institutions with the goal of minimizing credit risk. Banks that operate internationally are required to maintain a minimum amount (8%) of capital based on a percent of risk-weighted assets.

Capital Note: The subordinated security in the liability structure of a structured investment vehicle (SIV).

Captive Finance Company: A company that finances dealer inventories or consumer purchases of their products – usually affiliated with automotive or other manufacturing companies.

Collateralized Debt Obligation (CDO): A special purpose entity set up to own a pool of securities or loans, divide the pool's cash flows into tranches based on risk, and sell investors bonds that represent an interest in a particular tranche. The securities may be mortgage-backed securities or other similar securities. The tranches are designed to redistribute the risk of default. "Senior" tranches are considered the safest. Interest and principal payments are generally made in order of seniority, so that junior tranches offer higher coupon payments to compensate for additional default risk. CDOs are a type of structured debt.

Commercial Finance Company: A non-depository financial institution that makes asset based loans (such as for buying inventory, machines and equipment, vehicles) and enters into leasing arrangements.

Commercial Paper (CP): A short-term, unsecured promissory note issued by a large bank or corporation or a foreign government. The typical maturity is 1 to 270 days. As the note is backed only by the issuer's promise to pay, only firms with good credit ratings are able to issue unsecured commercial paper.

Consumer Finance Company: A non-depository lender that typically makes loans to consumers for furniture, appliances, and other purchases along with offering credit cards.

Credit Default Swap (CDS): A contract that promises payments triggered by a specific credit event. The buyer of the swap makes periodic payments to the seller of the swap in return for protection against a possible default affecting the value of a specified asset. The seller agrees to buy the specified asset from the buyer at par in the event of a credit default. The asset is typically some type of security, such as a corporate bond, CDO, or mortgage-backed security.

Credit Risk Transfer: The movement of assets off of balance sheets, often with the aim of easing capital requirements for firms.

Enhanced Cash Fund: Bond funds similar to money market funds, in that they aim to provide liquidity and principal preservation, but which: aim for higher returns, have less liquidity, invest in a wider variety of assets, and are not subject to certain SEC restrictions (such as SEC Rule 2a7).

Exchange Rate Swap: A simultaneous purchase and sale of identical amounts of one currency for another with two different value dates.

Financial Intermediation: The process of transforming the risk and/or timing of cash flows between savers and borrowers.

Glass-Steagall Act of 1933: Part of the Banking Act of 1933, Glass-Steagall mandated the separation of commercial banking from investment banking in order to address stock market speculation, self-dealing (using clients' funds for personal gain), and other abuses.

Gramm-Leach-Bliley Act of 1999 (GLBA): Also known as the Financial Services Modernization Act, it repealed the limitations on affiliations contained in the Glass-Steagall Act. Under GLBA, bank holding companies that meet certain capital, managerial, and other requirements may elect to become financial holding companies and thereby engage in a wider range of financial activities than they could otherwise, including full-scope securities underwriting, merchant banking, and insurance underwriting and sales.

Haircut: The difference between the market value of a security and the amount of money a lender will advance against it. The haircut acts as a buffer for absorbing any decline in the collateral's value in the event the loan is not repaid.

Interest Rate Swap: An agreement between two parties where one stream of future interest payments is exchanged for another based on a specified principal amount. Interest rate swaps often exchange a fixed payment for a floating payment that is linked to an interest rate (most often the LIBOR).

Investment Company Act of 1940: Created by Congress in 1940 and enforced and regulated by the Securities and Exchange Commission, this act clearly sets out the limits regarding filings, service charges, financial disclosure and fiduciary duties of open-end mutual, exchange-traded and closed-end funds.

Liquidity Risk: The risk stemming from the lack of marketability of an investment that cannot be bought or sold quickly enough to prevent or minimize a loss.

Local Government Investment Pool (LGIP): A state or local government pool offered to public entities for the investment of public funds.

Maturity Transformation: An aspect of financial intermediation, involving the issuance of short-term liabilities such as deposits to fund long-term assets such as mortgages.

Medium-Term Note (MTN): A debt note that usually matures in 5–10 years and can be issued on a fixed or floating coupon basis.

Money Market: The wholesale market for low-risk, highly liquid, short-term debt, such as U.S. Treasury bills, agency securities, commercial paper, certificates of deposit, and repos.

Money Market Fund (MMF): A mutual fund (SEC-registered investment fund) that is registered under Rule2a-7 of the Investment Company Act of 1940.

National Currency Act of 1863: Law establishing a national currency and a new government agency, the Office of the Comptroller of the Currency, to charter and supervise a new system of national banks.

Net Asset Value (NAV): A mutual fund's price per share.

Novation: The substitution of a new contract for an old one; or the substitution of one party in a contract with another party.

Repurchase Agreement (Repo): The sale of securities to an investor with an agreement to repurchase the securities at an agreed upon price and date. The Federal Reserve Bank of New York's Trading Desk uses repos of eligible securities to vary the quantity of banking system reserves as part of its implementation of monetary policy.

Shadow Banking: Refers to bank-like financial activities that are conducted by unregulated or lightly regulated institutions outside the traditional banking system.

Short Term Investment Fund (STIF): A type of fund that invests in short-term investments of high quality and low risk. The goal of this type of fund is to protect capital with low-risk investments while achieving a return that beats a relevant benchmark such as a Treasury bill index.

Special Purpose Entity (SPE): A legal entity (usually a limited liability company) created to fulfill a narrow or temporary objective. The SPV typically holds a portfolio of assets such as mortgage-backed securities or other debt obligations. The SPV exists to hold the assets and issue a new set of claims on the assets, making the sponsor of the SPV remote from any bankruptcy associated with the SPV and from the accounting, tax, and regulatory consequences of the SPV's activities.

Sweep Account: A bank account that automatically transfers amounts that exceed (or fall short of) a certain level into a higher interest earning investment option at the close of each business day. Commonly, the excess cash is swept into money market funds.

Total Return Swap: A swap agreement in which one party makes payments based on a set rate, either fixed or variable, while the other party makes payments based on the return of an underlying asset, which includes both the income it generates and any capital gains. In total return swaps, the underlying asset, referred to as the reference asset, is usually an equity index, loans, or bonds. This asset is owned by the party receiving the set rate payment.

Traditional Collateral: Collateral that consists of U.S. Treasuries and agency securities.

Wrapping: Process by which financial guarantors (which typically have high credit ratings) guarantee the principal and interest of a bond. This serves to enhance the credit quality of an underlying bond.

End Notes

[1] Key terms are defined in the Glossary.

[2] Federal Reserve Board Flow of Funds data.

[3] This figure represents only repo borrowing by broker-dealers, not repo borrowing by clients of the broker-dealers. Some research suggests that the total repo market may be substantially larger.

[4] Federal Reserve Board Flow of Funds data.

[5] Bank for International Settlements, *OTC derivatives market activity in the first half of2009*, November 2009. The notional value of a derivative is the nominal value of the contract, i.e. the amount on which the payments are calculated. The notional value does not ordinarily change hands. The gross market value of a derivative is the price at which the derivative trades.

[6] The securitization process is described in more detail in the FCIC Preliminary Staff Report, *Securitization and the Mortgage Crisis.*

[7] Additional mortgage debt was held in the GSE portfolios, at finance companies, and by other entities.

[8] The term "shadow banking system" was coined by PIMCO Managing Director Paul McCulley at the 2007 Jackson Hole Conference, sponsored by the Federal Reserve Bank of Kansas City; it has become part of the vernacular of the crisis. McCulley, *Teton Reflections*, August/September 2007.

[9] Testimony of Secretary Timothy Geithner before the House Financial Services Committee, April 20, 2010.

[10] The original act, as amended in 1935, did not disturb the power of banks to underwrite U.S. government securities and trade these securities for clients; it did, however, provide that a bank could not itself underwrite or deal in most other securities, for example, commercial paper, equity securities, or municipal revenue bonds, or be affiliated with a company "principally engaged" in such activities. See the FCIC Preliminary Staff Report, *The Role of the Federal Reserve in Banking Supervision and Regulation*.

[11] The Federal Reserve's Regulation Q continues to prohibit banks from paying interest on demand deposits, under Section 11 of the Glass-Steagall Act (12 U.S.C. 371a).

[12] In a 2005 report, international bank supervisors noted that credit derivatives and CDOs helped provide liquid and transparent markets for the trading of credit risk. The report also noted that credit risk transfer mechanisms could lead to growing concentrations of risk, for example in monoline financial guarantors. See Joint Forum (2005) and Joint Forum (2008).

[13] Firms may wish to hold less capital because capital held in reserve is not put to work purchasing profit-making assets.

[14] Board of Governors of the Federal Reserve System, *SR 05-6: Risk-Based Capital Treatment for Unrated Direct Credit Substitutes Extended to Asset-Backed Commercial Paper Programs*, March 30, 2005.

[15] Two observers have noted: "Banks exploited the fact that they could... get capital relief by simply switching away from loans into investments in the form of AAA-rated tranches of CDOs [collateralized debt obligations] and CLOs [collateralized loan obligations], which ... had a significantly lower capital charge. As a result, about 50 percent of all AAA asset-backed securities remained *within* the banking system." Viral V. Acharya and Philipp Schnabl, "How Banks Played the Leverage Game," in Acharya and Richardson (2009).

[16] The Federal Reserve has since the crisis taken a more aggressive supervisory approach to nonbanking subsidiaries.

[17] The CSE program was motivated, in part, to allow US investment banks to do business in Europe. Under the European Union's Financial Conglomerates Directive, non-EU financial institutions were essentially required to be supervised on a consolidated basis in order to do business in the EU, prompting the creation of the CSE program and the investment banks' voluntary enrollment. (Testimony by Erik Sirri, October 4, 2007; SEC (2008)).

[18] Net capital, for large firms, is a measure of equity that includes markdowns or "haircuts" based on the asset quality and liquidity of the firms' underlying assets. The net capital ratio divides net capital by aggregate outstanding debits.

[19] Basel Committee on Banking Supervision (2004).

[20] The SEC created the CSE program in response to a requirement by the European Union, in 2004, that foreign financial institutions operating in Europe must be subject to consolidated supervision in their home country. The CSE program was discontinued in 2008 after all five institutions had failed, been acquired by commercial bank holding companies, or become bank holding companies.

[21] SEC (2008).

[22] Chairman Ben Bernanke said recently: "Our supervisory approach should better reflect our mission, as a central bank, to promote financial stability. The extraordinary pressure on financial firms last fall underscored how profoundly interconnected firms and markets are in our complex, global financial system. Thus, any effort to address systemic risks will require a more systemwide, or macroprudential, approach to the supervision of systemically critical firms. More generally, supervisors must go beyond their traditional focus on individual firms and markets to try to identify possible channels of financial contagion and other risks to the system as a whole." Bernanke (2009).

[23] William Dudley, President of the Federal Reserve Bank of New York, recently said: "At its most fundamental level, this crisis was caused by the rapid growth of the so-called shadow banking system over the past few decades and its remarkable collapse over the past two years. ... Though the shadow banking system was often credited with better distributing risk and improving the overall efficiency of the financial system, this system ultimately proved to be much more fragile than we had anticipated. Like the traditional banking system, the shadow banking system engaged in the maturity transformation process in which structured investment vehicles (SIVs), conduits, dealers, and hedge funds financed long-term assets with short-term funding. However, much of the maturity transformation in the shadow system occurred without the types of stabilizing backstops that are in place in the traditional banking sector." Dudley (2009).

[24] These figures are computed as tangible assets over tangible equity, based on company regulatory data. Actual leverage was higher for the largest bank holding companies and investment banks when off-balance sheet commitments, including credit derivative exposures, were included.

[25] Pozsar (2008). Leverage will be the subject of a future FCIC staff report.

[26] Federal Reserve Board of Governors, *Commercial Bank Examination Manual*, October 2009, Section 2030.1, page 12.

[27] At the end of 2007, deposits comprised 72 percent of liabilities at commercial banks and thrifts. Retail deposits have been backed by the Federal Deposit Insurance Corporation (FDIC) since the banking runs of the 1930s. Each depositor is guaranteed to receive the full amount of his or her deposit up to $250,000 (increased during the current financial crisis from $100,000), regardless of the solvency of a commercial bank or savings institution. The figures cited do not include deposits at credit unions which are insured by the National Credit Union Share Insurance Fund.

[28] Note that thrifts owned by investment banks could access the Discount Window but those funds could not be used to support the parent company or any other subsidiary of the parent. The shadow banking system also did not have access to the lender-of-last-resort function of the Federal Home Loan Bank (FHLB) system, which issues federally guaranteed debt to purchase mortgages from savings and loan (thrift) institutions. During the second half of 2007, the FHLB system purchased $235 billion in mortgages from the thrifts when the securitization market froze. See Ashcraft, Bech, and Frame (2008).

[29] Crescenzi and Stigum (2007).

[30] Federal Reserve Board of Governor's commercial paper release and Securities Industry and Financial Markets Association (SIFMA) statistics.

[31] Money market mutual funds under Rule 2a-7 may hold up to five percent of assets in tier-1 securities issued by a single issuer and no more than one percent of assets in tier-2 securities issued by a single individual issuer. Also, tier-2 securities could not constitute more than five percent of assets at the time of the crisis.

[32] Federal Reserve Bank of New York Survey of Primary Dealers.

[33] Variable rate debt obligations and tender option bonds were similar short-term instruments used by municipalities to fund longer-term commitments.

[34] Investment Company Institute Money Market Working Group Report, 2009.

[35] The term "hedge fund" refers to the original strategy of investing in equities and using short-positions and leverage to hedge overall positions. There is no official regulatory definition.

[36] GAO (2008) for main figures. International Financial Services London says there are 11,000 funds with total assets of $2.25 trillion; Hennessee Group LLC estimates 9,550 funds as of early 2007 with assets of $1.9 trillion; Hedge Fund Research Inc. estimates 10,096 funds in second quarter 2007.

[37] GAO (2008).

[38] See Goldstein v Securities and Exchange Commission, 451 F.3[r]d 873 (D.C. Cir. 2006)

[39] For a complete discussion of the oversight of hedge funds, see GAO (2008).

[40] See the FCIC Preliminary Staff Report, *Government Sponsored Enterprises and the Financial Crisis.*

[41] Barth (2009), page 28.

[42] See the FCIC Preliminary Staff Report, *The Mortgage Crisis*.

[43] HSBC Finance Corp., *10-K 12/31/2006*, March 5, 2007, page 30.

[44] On March 22, the Senate Committee on Banking, Housing, and Urban Affairs, held a hearing to investigate the subprime mortgage industry, based on a report by a public advocacy

group that as many as 2.2 million subprime homeowners would lose their homes in the coming crisis. Center for Responsible Lending (2006).

[45] Paul Muolo and Mathew Padilla, *Chain ofBlame*, 2008, page 177.

[46] Khandani and Lo (2007).

[47] An interest rate spread is the difference between two rates and measures the relative riskiness of the assets, rather than changes in the level of market interest rates. ABCP and financial CP spreads to nonfinancial CP reflect investors' perceptions of risk across types of commercial paper, and are a standard metric of the health and operation of those markets.

[48] Covitz, Liang, and Suarez (2009).

[49] Moody's (2007a, 2007b).

[50] Contrary to market fears at the time, it eventually turned out that the unwinding of the SIVs was not detrimental. "SIVs suffered a variety of fates. Of the 29 SIVs: five were restructured; seven defaulted on payments to their senior notes; 13 were supported by the sponsoring bank – a number of which have since delevered; and Fitch estimates that the remaining four SIVs have also delevered." See Fitch (2009).

[51] Covitz, Liang and Suarez (2009).

[52] SIGTARP, *Quarterly Report to Congress*, July 21, 2009, pp. 141-142.

[53] Moody's Investors Service, *Moody's announces rating actions on financial guarantors*, December 14, 2007; Standard & Poor's Ratings Services, *S&P Takes Rating Actions On Six Bond Insurers*, December 19, 2007.

[54] Fitch Ratings, *Fitch Downgrades Ambac; Ratings Remain on Watch Negative*, January 18, 2008.

[55] Moody's Investors Service, *Moody's confirms MBIA's Aaa rating, changes outlook to negative*, February 26, 2008, and *Moody's confirms Ambac's Aaa rating; changes outlook to negative*, March 12, 2008.

[56] Standard & Poor's Ratings Services, *S&P Takes Additional Bond Insurer Rating Actions*, February 25, 2008.

[57] Han and Li (2009).

[58] The firm had been under pressure for some time since the BSAM funds went bankrupt. Importantly, the maturity of its repo obligations had shortened as counterparties became less willing to provide long-term funds.

[59] In a novation, a party that wants to exit its trade position with a counterparty (for example, Bear), assigns or novates the position to a new counterparty. The former counterparty (Bear) grants consent to the novation, which essentially takes it out of the trade.

[60] Senior Supervisors Group (2009).

In: Shadow Banking and Its Role ... ISBN: 978-1- 62081-703-2
Editors: D. A. Jenkins and M. I. Collins

Chapter 2

TESTIMONY OF TIMOTHY F. GEITHNER, SECRETARY, U.S. DEPARTMENT OF THE TREASURY. HEARING ON "THE SHADOW BANKING SYSTEM"*

Chairman Angelides, Vice Chairman Thomas, members of the Commission, thank you for the opportunity to testify.

Nearly eight decades ago, after a series of banking crises led to the Great Depression, the United States put in place broad protections over the financial system. These reforms – deposit insurance, prudential rules to limit risk-taking by banks, and improved transparency and investor protection in our securities markets – alongside the Federal Reserve's role as lender of last resort, laid the foundation for a more stable banking industry for several decades.

Over time, however, the financial system outgrew those protections. A large parallel financial system emerged outside of the framework of protections established for traditional banks. A great diversity of financial institutions emerged to provide banking services to individuals and companies, and they were allowed to operate without being subject to the same constraints applied to traditional banks. The shift in mortgage lending away from banks, the growth of the relative importance of non bank financial institutions, the increase in the size of investment banks, and the emergence of a range of specialized financing vehicles are all manifestations of this phenomenon.

---

* This is an edited, reformatted and augmented version of testimony given on May 6, 2010, before the Financial Crisis Inquiry Commission.

The growth of this parallel financial system was made possible in part, and proved more damaging, because of a long period of relative economic and financial stability, encouraging borrowers and investors to take on more risk. Across the U.S. economy and around the world, trillions of dollars of financial decisions were made on the expectation that U.S. house prices would never fall, that future recessions would be short and shallow, that systemic crises in developed markets were a thing of the past, that liquidity and funding would be always available, and that the world economy would continue to grow unabated.

These judgments proved to be too optimistic. The entire financial system, and the borrowers and investors it served, did not attach enough importance to the possibility of a severe crisis. The protections put in place over the traditional banking system did not provide sufficient financial cushions or shock absorbers to withstand a deep recession and a substantial fall in real estate values. The parallel financial system, operating with much weaker protections, was even more vulnerable.

That is the story of this financial crisis. And addressing these failures is an essential part of the comprehensive financial reforms now being considered by the Congress.

The Emergence of the Parallel Banking System and Its Consequences

While the term "shadow banking" has been given different meanings in different contexts, we use it to describe the network of institutions and financial activities that provide basic banking-type services outside the scope of classic banking regulation.

At its core, banking is the business of taking deposits from "savers" and lending those deposits to borrowers. The basic tension in this business was perhaps best described by Jimmy Stewart in "It's A Wonderful Life" when facing a run on his bank. Stewart responds to a depositor who wants to withdraw his savings, "...the money's not here...your money's in Joe's house...and in the Kennedy House, and Mrs. Macklin's house, and, and a hundred others..." The challenge of banking is managing the mismatch between the needs of depositors who can demand their money at any time, and those of borrowers who take out a loan with no obligation to repay the funds for months or years.

The modern policy framework for banking emerged in the 1930s to address that inherent instability. It provides banks with lender-of-last-resort privileges and, for a fee, access to federal deposit insurance. But this support does not come without cost. It creates moral hazard and encourages banks to take excessive risks. Our regulatory system, which includes activity restrictions, capital requirements, and prudential supervision for banks is designed in part to constrain that excessive risk-taking.

But this regulatory system did not evolve to keep pace with growth and innovations in our financial services industry. The constraints imposed by banking regulation were significant enough to encourage activity to move away from banks in search of lighter regulation, lower capital requirements, weaker consumer protections, and better tax and accounting treatment.

Over time, the size of this parallel banking system grew to the point where it was almost as large as the entire traditional banking system. At its peak, this alternative banking system financed about $8 trillion in assets. Many of these assets were financed with short-term obligations and in institutions or funding vehicles with substantial leverage – leaving them with relatively thin cushions of resources to protect against the possibility of loss.

This parallel system came in many shapes and sizes. Independent investment banks like Lehman Brothers and Bear Stearns grew in size and financed themselves in the overnight repurchase agreement, or "repo" markets, which rely on assets or securities as collateral. Asset-backed commercial paper (ABCP) conduits and structured investment vehicles (SIVs) were used by banks and a broad range of other financial institutions as funding vehicles for different types of assets. Specialized finance companies expanded into a broad range of consumer and business lending activities.

These institutions and funds were financed by institutional investors and by money market mutual funds, which purchased their short term commercial paper, or lent to them overnight in the repo markets secured by various forms of collateral.

Across this system, longer-term financial assets, which necessarily had some risk of loss, were financed short term, by investors and funds that had the right to withdraw their money or refuse to continue to fund a maturing obligation.

This parallel system was particularly vulnerable to a classic run or banking panic. As the crisis intensified, investors began to pull back. This forced institutions in the parallel financial system to sell assets to meet those demands. That pushed the price of financial assets down further, leading to more pressure on those institutions.

Unlike a traditional bank run, which is visible in lines outside of banks as people rush to withdraw their money ahead of a collapse, this run was led by institutional investors managing mutual funds and pension funds.

The confidence investors had in the value or assigned rating of the collateral backing their loans or investments evaporated. While this panic might have been less visible than in the panics of years past, it was no less real.

As a result of this run, aggressive policy measures were required to prevent a second Great Depression. The Federal Reserve, acting under its emergency authorities, launched an unprecedented expansion of support to preserve liquidity in the parallel banking sector, lending against collateral held by primary dealers in investment banks, providing a backstop to commercial paper markets. The Treasury Department used its existing authority to supply a temporary guarantee of the money market fund industry.

The FDIC implemented additional liquidity measures to stabilize the funding base of the regulated banking system, including a debt guarantee program and significant expansions of deposit insurance. Congress enacted the Emergency Economic Stabilization Act, making it possible for the Treasury Department to make preferred equity investments in banks across the country.

How Did This Happen?

Despite the fact that many call this the shadow banking system, it was not hidden. It was operating in broad daylight and financed by sophisticated institutional investors with bonds issued under the disclosures and protections of the securities laws.

And unlike the moral hazard risk in banks and the GSEs, this market grew up without any explicit or implicit government insurance or any history of government support in a crisis. This was a pure failure of market discipline.

Why did the system of oversight in place for decades following the Great Depression not protect against the growth of risk in this parallel system?

The history of this crisis is full of examples where regulators did not use the authority they had early enough or strongly enough to contain risks in the system. But a principal cause of the crisis was the failure to provide legal authority to constrain risk in this parallel financial system.

Prudential regulations were limited to banks, and did not extend to the parallel financial system.

The Federal Reserve did not have any legal authority to set and enforce capital requirements on the major institutions that operated banking businesses outside of bank holding companies, no legal authority over the investment banks, diversified financial institutions like AIG, or the hundreds of non bank finance companies competing with banks in the mortgage, consumer credit, and business lending markets.

The SEC had no legal authority to set and enforce capital requirements on a consolidated basis across the full range of activities of the investment banks.

The Office of Thrift Supervision became the holding company supervisor for an array of large complicated financial institutions like AIG, without having the ability to supervise them effectively on a consolidated basis.

No single entity had the authority to act to limit the emerging risk in funding markets financed by money market funds.

No regulator or supervisor had the legal authority to look across the financial system and take action to prevent the diversion of activity away from regulation. A system that applied safety and soundness regulation only to banks was unable to protect the overall safety and stability of a financial system composed substantially of non-banks that played a role traditionally reserved for banks.

Moreover, accounting and disclosure requirements and regulatory capital requirements helped encourage the shift in risk to the parallel financial system, without adequately capturing the remaining exposure of banks to those risks.

When the crisis hit and huge swaths of the American financial system got caught in the run on the parallel banking system, many came running to the Federal Reserve for liquidity and for protection.

The emergency financial response to the run that started in the parallel financial system was necessary to protect our economy from an even greater calamity. But if our regulatory and supervisory systems had had the tools and authorities to prevent risks from accumulating in unregulated sectors of the financials system in the first place, such a large emergency response would not have been necessary. That is a key reason why financial reform is so essential.

Financial Reform

The financial reform proposals now being considered by the Congress have been crafted to address these and other failures and they are being complemented by enhanced regulatory oversight of key aspects of the shadow banking system.

- *Comprehensive Constraints on Risk Taking.* The proposed reforms will require the enforcement of more conservative capital and leverage requirements on the activities, whether on or off balance sheet, of all major financial institutions. A company like AIG or Lehman Brothers will not be able to escape consolidated supervision by virtue of its corporate form, and will have to operate on a level playing field with large commercial banks and traditionally regulated financial institutions.
- *Repo Markets.* These reforms will give the Federal Reserve the authority to build a more stable funding system, take action to address the unstable aspects of the short-term repo markets, and ensure that these markets are used much more conservatively in the future. These steps will give clear authority to set risk management requirements for these markets, including capital standards, set standards for collateral requirements, and to help ensure that settlement procedures are robust. They will also create enforcement authority to compel corrective actions as risks build up, or when risk-management is inadequate. These authorities will also reinforce stability and liquidity even in times of market stress such as a terrorist attack or acute financial crisis.
- *Higher Standards for Money Market Mutual Funds.* The SEC recently enacted new rules to strengthen liquidity, credit standards and disclosure in the money fund industry. More work remains to be done in this area, and the President's Working Group on Financial Markets is preparing a report setting forth options to reduce the susceptibility of money funds to runs.
- *Rating Agencies, Disclosure, and Accounting.* These reforms will provide the SEC with authority to limit conflicts of interest, require greater disclosure to ensure more diversity in ratings, and require regulators to reduce the overall reliance on ratings throughout the supervisory system. The SEC will require more extensive disclosure, including loan-level data for asset-back securities, to ensure that investors have the information they need to make informed decisions. Changes underway to accounting standards will result in greater transparency for a firm's off-balance sheet commitments, improve standards, and move forward international accounting convergence.
- *Derivatives.* These reforms will bring comprehensive oversight and transparency to the OTC derivatives markets. These markets have proved to be a major source of uncertainty and risk during periods of

financial disruption. The proposed reforms will bring the bulk of these trades into central clearing arrangements, ensuring full transparency and reducing the degree to which financial contagion can spread due to real or perceived counterparty credit exposures. All dealers and major market participants will be subject to tough prudential standards, including margin and capital requirements. And the SEC and CFTC will have full enforcement authority to set position limits and address fraud, manipulation, and abuse.

- *Resolution Authority.* These reforms will establish a resolution regime that will give the government the necessary tools to safely put failing financial institutions out of existence without causing a panic or destabilizing credit markets, and without exposing the tax payer to the risk of loss.

CONCLUSION

When people look back at this crisis, when they look at the excessive risks taken by large financial institutions, the natural inclination is to move those risky activities elsewhere. To create stability, some argue, we should just separate banks from "risk."

But, in important ways, that is exactly what caused this crisis.

The lesson of this crisis, and of the parallel financial system, is that we cannot make the economy safe by taking functions central to the business of banking, functions necessary to help raise capital for businesses and help businesses hedge risk, and move them outside banks, and outside the reach of strong regulation.

Mr. Chairman, let me close by thanking the Commission for your important work in drawing public attention to one of the key factors in this crisis, and one of the most important objectives of financial reform.

In: Shadow Banking and Its Role ... ISBN: 978-1- 62081-703-2
Editors: D. A. Jenkins and M. I. Collins

Chapter 3

TESTIMONY OF HENRY M. PAULSON, JR., FORMER SECRETARY, U.S. DEPARTMENT OF THE TREASURY. HEARING ON "THE SHADOW BANKING SYSTEM"*

Chairman Angelides, Vice Chairman Thomas, and members of the Commission, thank you for the opportunity to testify today.

I served as Secretary of the Treasury during the recent financial crisis. I am proud of the work we in government did to save our nation's financial system from collapse and chaos, and our economy from disaster. Even so, the crisis caused human suffering that simply cannot be measured. The American people deserve—and policymakers will benefit from—an understanding of the broad and diverse causes of the crisis. The job of providing that explanation falls to this Commission, and it is an awesome responsibility.

Many mistakes were made by all market participants, including financial institutions, investors, regulators, and the rating agencies, as well as by policy makers. Most of these are well understood, and, importantly, policymakers are currently addressing some major regulatory structure and authority issues that either allowed the pre-2007 excesses in our system or made it difficult to address the crisis. Nonetheless a number of the root causes are not being addressed and remain sources of danger to our country.

I fully support your important mission, and I hope that my testimony today can assist it. I will start by giving my views on the fundamental causes

* This is an edited, reformatted and augmented version of testimony given on May 6, 2010, before the Financial Crisis Inquiry Commission.

of the financial crisis, and then turn to the specific topic of today's hearing—the so-called "shadow banking" system. My views are based on my long experience in the financial markets, my time as Secretary of the Treasury during the financial crisis, and the consideration I have given to these issues in the year-and-a-half since I left government.

***

The roots of the financial crisis trace back to several factors, including housing policy, global capital flows, over-leveraged financial institutions, poor consumer protection, and an archaic and outmoded financial regulatory system—among many other causes.

Underlying the crisis was the housing bubble, and it is clear that several policy decisions shaped the home mortgage market. Excesses in that market eventually led to a significant decline in home prices and a surge of loan defaults which caused tremendous losses in the financial system, triggered a contraction of credit, and put many Americans—quite literally—out on the street. These excesses were driven in large part by housing policy. From 1994 to 2006, home ownership soared from an already spectacular 64 percent of U.S. households to a staggering 69 percent due to the combined weight of a number of government policies and programs. Fannie Mae and Freddie Mac, the government sponsored enterprises (GSEs) comprised a central part of U.S. housing policy. The GSEs operated under an inherently flawed model of private profit backed by public support, which encouraged risky revenue seeking and ultimately led to significant taxpayer losses.

The United States has always encouraged home ownership, and rightly so. Home ownership builds wealth, stabilizes neighborhoods, creates jobs, and promotes economic growth. But it must be pursued responsibly. The right person must be matched to the right house (and consequently the right home loan), and in the years before the crisis we lost that discipline.

The overstimulation of the housing market caused by government policy was exacerbated by other problems in that market. Subprime mortgages went from accounting for 5 percent of total mortgages in 1994 to 20 percent by 2006. Consumer protection, including state regulation of mortgage originations, was spotty, inconsistent, and, in some cases, nonexistent. Speculation on rising home prices led to increasingly risky loans, including far too many home loans made with no money down. Securitization separated originators from the risk of the products they originated. Mortgage fraud increased, and predatory lenders and unscrupulous brokers pushed increasingly complex mortgages onto unsuspecting borrowers. The result was a housing bubble that eventually burst in far more spectacular fashion than most previous bubbles.

Global forces also played a significant role in causing the crisis. Imbalances in the world's economies led to massive and destabilizing cross-border capital flows. While other nations save, Americans spend. Consumption in this country is the norm, spurred on by low interest rates aided by capital flowing from countries, notably China and Japan, which have high savings and low shares of domestic consumption, and further encouraged by U.S. tax laws that discourage saving. We were living beyond our means, on borrowed money and borrowed time. Consumers, businesses, and financial institutions all overextended and overleveraged themselves with inevitably disastrous results while our federal and state governments continued to borrow heavily, jeopardizing their long-term fiscal flexibility.

Our financial institutions—including commercial and investment banks—were notable examples of this overleveraging. In general, these institutions did not maintain sufficient, high-quality capital, which left them unable to absorb the significant losses they incurred as the housing bubble burst. Many of them did not understand their liquidity positions fully. They held insufficient cash and cash equivalents, and instead relied overly on short term funding sources that ran dry as the credit markets contracted. These leverage problems were further exacerbated by a lack of transparency, which caused problems in subprime to infect other classes of assets. Like a tainted food scare, a relatively small batch of deadly products—securitized subprime mortgages—led to fear and panic in the markets for many mortgage securitizations, driving down the price of assets, which triggered huge losses and severe liquidity problems. Derivative contracts, including excessively complex financial products, exacerbated the problem. These instruments embedded leverage in institutions' balances sheets along with risks which were so obscured that at times they were not fully understood by investors, creditors, rating agencies, regulators, or the management themselves. Very importantly, a number of financial institutions had woefully inadequate risk management and liquidity management practices that allowed these problems to grow and intensify, in a number of cases leading to failure of the institution.

Compounding the problems at these financial institutions was a financial regulatory system that was archaic and outmoded. Our regulatory framework was built at a different time for a different system, and it has not kept pace with the rapid changes in the financial industry. I noted during my time at Treasury the enormous gaps in authority, duplication of responsibility, and unhealthy jurisdictional competition. No single regulator had responsibility for overseeing the stability of the system. The result was that regulators were often unable to supervise the firms they oversaw adequately, they did not see the impending systemic problems that progressed towards a crisis, and they did not have the tools to contain all the harms that unfolded as institutions began to collapse. In March of 2008, this led me to recommend a blueprint for major reform of our financial regulatory system after a year-long comprehensive review.

***

I will turn now to the specific topic of today's hearing: the "shadow banking" system, a term that refers to the large capital and credit markets outside the traditional banking system that provide credit for municipal governments, corporations, and individuals for short, intermediate, and long term funding needs. Before the crisis, these markets satisfied at least half of consumer and business credit needs and are one of the hallmarks of our advanced and highly developed capital markets. They have greatly benefited our nation, spurring growth and prosperity at all levels of our economy. They have enabled more people to receive higher education, more people to purchase homes, more people to start new businesses, and more people to plan effectively for their children's future. They have increased consumer choice, stimulated job creation, and allowed our system to diversify away from the large, concentrated banks found in other capital markets.

But like all activities in the financial sector, these markets were fueled by the global excesses and regulatory flaws I have already discussed. Inside and outside the traditional banking system, financial institutions overreached, financial services were misused, and financial products were misunderstood. In addition, our regulatory system was balkanized, outdated, and lacked the infrastructure to oversee these markets, something I had observed and attempted to reform throughout my tenure at Treasury. When the crisis hit, the stress it placed on these markets exposed many of these flaws, and these flaws in turn extended and exacerbated some of the effects of the crisis.

These problems must be addressed. Our financial system cannot move forward without fortifying the weak parts of its infrastructure. But in addressing these problems, we must make sure we retain the benefits of the underlying financial innovations. In our haste to deal with the flaws in the non-bank financial system, we should not move ourselves back to a system of consolidated, monolithic commercial banks. I am confident that a thoughtful process can achieve this.

I will provide a few examples of areas in the non-bank financial system where flaws were exposed by the recent crisis, but that can, in my view, continue to function productively with appropriate regulation and oversight. Some of these suggestions I put forward while I was at Treasury—both before and after the crisis. Others are based on my study and reflection in the time since I left government.

SECURITIZATION

Securitization is the process by which a collection of assets—for example, mortgages, car loans, or credit card receivables—are packaged together by an underwriter and then sold to a large group of diversified investors. Because securitization separated mortgage originators and underwriters from holding the risk of the loans they originate, it enabled subprime lenders to stop focusing on the creditworthiness of the loans they made, and instead focus solely on their ability to sell those loans upstream to underwriters. Underwriters in turn relaxed their underwriting criteria, relying on their ability to sell their securities into a booming market. Investors did not do due diligence on these investments, instead allowing their judgment to be guided by exuberant ratings agencies and risk sensibilities dulled by the benign market conditions and the complexity of novel financial instruments.

But securitization is not, in and of itself a bad thing. Proper securitization has greatly expanded the credit available to responsible consumers, by allowing loans that large commercial banks find unprofitable to be diversified among numerous financial institutions. A large amount of the credit available to consumers comes from this important market, including such useful products as credit cards, student loans, and small business loans. And, as we saw in the recent crisis, the functioning of these markets is critical to our economic success. In 2008, when the problems in the mortgage securitization market caused other securitization markets to grind to a halt, consumers and business found themselves choked off from funds, and productivity and prosperity soon declined.

That being said, reforms are unquestionably required. Better disclosure is necessary. Underwriters and originators should be required to retain some portion of what they sell. Requiring underwriters to keep some "skin in the game" will properly align their incentives with those of investors who end up holding the bulk of the risk. In addition, we must reform and strengthen oversight of rating agencies and eliminate those areas of our securities regulations and laws that reference third-party ratings, which have tended to serve as a crutch or an excuse, discouraging investors and regulators from doing the necessary credit analysis. These changes will provide the securitization market with powerful incentives to focus on creditworthiness and will lead to more responsible lending practices.

Repurchase Agreements

The repurchase agreement market is a major source of funding for financial institutions. A repurchase agreement—or "repo"—is essentially a form of short term secured lending. One institution sells a security—such as a Treasury bond, agency debt, or mortgage-backed security—to a counterparty for cash, and agrees to buy it back later, typically the following day, at the same price, plus interest. Institutions may engage in repos directly with one another or through a third-party intermediary who administers the transaction and serves as custodian of the securities being transacted—a so-called "tri-party repo" transaction.

By the time the crisis hit, the repo market had grown to an enormous size at an astonishing speed. Architecture, infrastructure, and regulation had not kept up. Lending practices had become sloppy, lenders vastly expanded the collateral they would lend against, without demanding sufficient protection, and no single regulator had the necessary information and the authority for dealing with the attendant problems. Partly as a result, many firms placed too much faith in the market's seemingly constant supply of easy liquidity. When the crisis hit, these problems came home to roost as the markets declined. Lenders became increasingly strict about the types of collateral they would accept, and borrowers consequently found their access to liquidity evaporating. Bear Stearns, for example, which relied heavily on tri-party repo to meet short term funding needs, saw its cash on hand drop from $18 billion to $2 billion in the few days before its rescue, due in part to its loss of access to the repo markets. The crisis of 2008 was characterized by a run on the secured borrowing of a number of financial institutions.

I believe the repo market can, and should, be able to function efficiently while serving us better during future periods of market stress. It makes sense for firms to be able to use their securities as collateral to fulfill certain short term funding needs, rather than being required to always obtain wholesale credit from large banks. For this to work, however, the market must be well supported by a robust infrastructure, appropriate technology, and intelligent oversight.

For example, the Federal Reserve has sponsored an industry-led task for to develop enhancements to the policies, procedures, and systems that support the tri-party repo market, and I look forward to the results of those efforts, some of which should also be applicable to the broader repo market. In addition, the crisis has underscored the point that, even in a well functioning market, firms cannot rely on short-term funding in place of proper liquidity management.

COMMERCIAL PAPER

Commercial paper refers to unsecured notes sold to investors outside of the banking system. These notes are very short term, with maturities from one day to not more than a few months.

A variety of institutions relied on commercial paper for their funding. For example, large businesses used it as a means of obtaining short term financing based on their credit ratings. Financial institutions used it as a means to fund securitizations, so-called "asset backed commercial paper," sometimes off balance sheet.

The financial crisis exposed weaknesses in this market. As the financial industry came under stress, investors pulled back from the market, and when Lehman collapsed, even major industrial corporations found it difficult to sell their paper.

The resulting liquidity crunch, showed that firms had overly relied on this short term funding and had failed to anticipate how restricted the commercial paper market could become in times of stress.

That said, the commercial paper market remains tremendously valuable. It has functioned effectively and transparently for a long time, proving a useful source of short term funding to many major industrial and financial firms and a stable, relatively liquid investment for money market funds and other large investors. But financial institutions and their regulators must be aware of the risks associated with its use.

It should be used to fund short-term requirements only and even then not be a disproportionate part of a firm's liability profile. Importantly, all commercial paper issuance should be backed up by bank lines of credit to provide greater stability to the market in times of stress.

DERIVATIVES

Derivative contracts—including credit default swaps—serve a useful function in mitigating risk and making the capital markets more efficient. They did not cause the crisis, but they did introduce greater interconnectedness as well as embedded and hidden leverage into financial institutions' balance sheets, and, in many instances, they magnified the effects of other risks. For example, AIG, by serving as a counterparty to numerous credit default swap contracts, exposed itself to tremendous risk in the mortgage market and threatened the entire financial system with its potential failure, all while escaping the notice of regulators.

Better regulation of these products is clearly needed. Standardized derivatives should be traded on a public exchange, and nonstandardized contracts should be centrally cleared and should be subject to more regulatory scrutiny, transparency, and greater capital charges. Such regulations will encourage standardization, promote transparency, and penalize excessive complexity with capital charges, thereby restoring these products to their proper function—mitigating, not enhancing, risk.

MONEY MARKET MUTUAL FUNDS

Money market funds are an enormous industry, managing nearly $4 trillion in assets for over 30 million customers. These funds invest primarily in government securities and top rated commercial paper. Before the crisis, investors had come to believe that investing in these funds guaranteed them their principal back and complete liquidity, because the funds would always maintain a net asset value (NAV) of at least $1.00. In the immediate aftermath of the Lehman failure, money market mutual funds came under intense pressure, eroding investor confidence and causing redemption requests to soar. The money market funds in turn began to pull back on their commercial paper investments causing funding to dry up for those institutions that relied on that market for liquidity needs. Disaster was averted when we stepped in and guaranteed the funds in order to prevent the crisis from worsening.

I continue to think that these funds are great products and have the ability to offer consumers attractive returns, liquidity, and very low volatility and principal risk. But the expectation that these funds can provide better yields than Treasury bills or insured deposits, and at the same time provide complete liquidity and no loss of principal, is unrealistic. Consumers must be disabused of that notion for the market to thrive. To that end, the SEC has recently enacted new rules governing disclosure in this industry. I suggest that the SEC also explore whether fund managers should move from a fixed NAV, which makes money market funds resemble insured bank accounts, to a floating NAV. The funds would still provide great value, but as clients saw slight variations in principal, they would have a tangible indication that they were not investing in a bank account.

***

The innovations of our modern financial system should be a source of pride. They are expressions of American ingenuity and inventiveness, and they will help secure our rightful place as a leader in the global economy. They also deserve thoughtful scrutiny and appropriate regulation, as they must be well understood and properly used. I am confident that the Commission, as it examines these issues in light of the recent crisis, will properly balance these important considerations.

Thank you, and I would be pleased to answer any questions.

In: Shadow Banking and Its Role ... ISBN: 978-1- 62081-703-2
Editors: D. A. Jenkins and M. I. Collins

Chapter 4

STATEMENT OF PAUL A. MCCULLEY, MANAGING DIRECTOR, PIMCO. HEARING ON "THE SHADOW BANKING SYSTEM"*

Chairman Angelides, Vice-Chairman Thomas, and honorable Members of the Commission, my name is Paul McCulley and I am a managing director and portfolio manager with PIMCO. On behalf of my colleagues at PIMCO, I thank you for the invitation to appear before this distinguished Commission today.

I am especially honored to be invited to testify at your hearings on the Shadow Banking System. My comments today will try to offer a framework for understanding the nature of the "shadow banking system," [1] and linking it to the core functions performed by the conventional banking system. I will conclude with some thoughts on lessons learned from the financial crisis.

Before I turn to this topic, I would like to provide a brief overview and background of PIMCO and my role with the firm. PIMCO is an investment management firm founded in 1971, based in Newport Beach, California. PIMCO employs approximately 1,300 people, some 900 of whom work in our two U.S. offices. We also have 9 offices outside of the U.S. PIMCO manages retirement and investment assets for more than 8 million people in the U.S. and millions more around the world. Our clients include pension funds that represent public sector employees at the state and local level, unions,

---

* This is an edited, reformatted and augmented version of a statement given on May 6, 2010, before the Financial Crisis Inquiry Commission.

universities, foundations, endowments and private companies that employ Americans from all walks of life.

Specifically, an investment manager is hired to invest money on behalf of clients based on contractual guidelines that they establish with us. Our objective is to protect and enhance our clients' assets and help them achieve their investment goals over time. We do not conduct investment banking or proprietary trading activities.

In terms of my role with PIMCO, I joined the firm in 1999 and serve as head of PIMCO's Short-Term Desk. I am also a member of the firm's Investment Committee and a generalist portfolio manager.

Let me now turn to the substantive issue that you have asked me to speak about today: the role of the shadow banking system in the financial crisis of 2007-2009.

THE SHADOW BANKING SYSTEM AND THE FINANCIAL CRISIS

Banking is fundamentally defined as the business of transforming savings into investment in our economy, while simultaneously acting as the nation's payments system. Traditionally, we think of this activity in the context of conventional banks, which issue deposits and then turn them into loans. Technically, this activity is called maturity, liquidity and quality transformation. Simply put, this means that banks transform their deposit base into loans that are of longer maturity, less liquidity and lower credit quality than their liabilities.

Historically, when Americans needed a loan for their home, business (and starting in the 20th century) automobile, or to help finance a child's college education, they would go to their neighborhood bank and borrow the funds from that institution. Structurally, and when conducted properly, this activity delivers value to the borrower in the form of funds that they do not currently have, and in return provides profit for the bank in terms of higher interest that the borrower pays for the loan than the bank pays depositors for their savings.

The defining characteristic of the system of banking from time immemorial rests on the proposition that the public's collective *ex ante* demand for an asset that trades at par on demand is greater than the public's *ex post* demand for such an asset. The system therefore necessarily requires faith on the part of depositors that their money is safe. Up through the early 20th century, banks in the U.S. were prone to runs because depositors did not have sufficient confidence in the banking system that they could get their money anytime they wanted at par.

Major Financial "Panics" of the 19th Century

Name	Cause
Panic of 1819	The Second Bank of the United States, worried about land speculation, abruptly reined in lending, causing a six-year depression.
Panic of 1837	The Specie Circular, under which the federal government would accept land payment only in gold and silver, helped start a run on banks and the failure of more than 800 of them.
Panic of 1857	Failure of the New York City branch of Ohio Life Insurance and Trust Co. led to bank runs and widespread bankruptcies.
Panic of 1873	Speculation in railroads led to the insolvency of Philadelphia bank Jay Cooke and Co. Eighty-nine of the nation's 364 railroads went bankrupt.
Panic of 1893	Controversy over the gold standard provoked "Industrial Black Friday" on the stock market. More than 500 banks and 16,000 businesses failed.

Source: Samuel Rezneck, *Business Depressions and Financial Panics: Collected Essays in American Business and Economic History* (1969), *available at* http://www.fdic.gov/ba nk/analytical/regional/ro20062q/na/2006_summer01.html.

Source: Gary Gorton, *Slapped in the Face by the Invisible Hand: Banking and the Panic of 2007* 3 (May 9, 2009), http://www.frbatlanta.org/news/CONFEREN /09fmc/gorton.pdf.

The cycle of bank runs in the 19th and early 20th centuries led Congress to enact legislation creating the Federal Reserve System in 1913 and the Federal Deposit Insurance Corporation in 1933, which, among other things, made it clear to the public that the U.S. Government was the lender of last resort; in other words that their money was safe at U.S.-insured banks.

The establishment of these backstops significantly diminished the frequency of bank runs because depositors did not feel it necessary to actually ask for their money. In the terminology of Professor Gary Gorton of Yale University, FDIC-insured deposits issued by banks with access to the Federal Reserve's discount window are "informationally insensitive." That is, holders of such deposits do not have to do any due diligence or gathering of information to feel comfortable holding such deposits. While technically they are the liability of the issuing bank, they are viewed by the public as backed by the full faith and credit of the government. While it is true that such backstops may increase moral hazard in the conventional banking system by eliminating the pressure on savers to carefully examine which banks they entrust with their money, these safeguards have enabled our economy to grow while limiting the volatility and significant economic costs caused by bank runs.

Since the creation of the Federal Reserve and the FDIC, conventional banking has inherently been a joint venture between the private sector and the public sector – deposits are made "informationally insensitive" to the public by the safety nets from the government, allowing conventional bankers to redeploy those deposits into longer dated, riskier loans and securities, earning a net interest margin.

Given the fact that conventional banking is indeed a joint venture between the private sector and the public sector, conventional banking has been regulated: if the public is responsible for underwriting deposit insurance, then the government rightfully imposes regulation regarding how banks operate, notably how much capital and liquidity they must hold, as well as the types of activities in which they may engage.

In recent decades, the shadow banking system developed to provide many of the same lending and intermediary functions of conventional banks, also sharing their same profit motive. Today, many Americans fund their home loans, car loans and student loans via institutions that are part of the shadow banking system, accessing funds from around the world through the securitization market.

One of the distinctions between shadow and conventional banks, however, is that while the latter are subject to an extensive regulatory framework, the former typically are not. To the extent there is an overarching 'regulatory' framework of the shadow banking system, the *de facto* regulators are the rating agencies.[2]

Outstanding Amounts Various Non-Mortgage Asset-Backed Securities ($bil.)							
	Automobile	Credit Card	Home Equity	Manufactured	Student		
	Loans	Receivables	Loans	Housing	Loans	Other	Total
1996	71.4	180.7	51.6	14.6	10.1	76.0	404.4
1997	77.0	214.5	90.2	19.1	18.3	116.7	535.8
1998	86.9	236.7	124.2	25.0	25.0	233.7	731.5
1999	114.1	257.9	141.9	33.8	36.4	316.7	900.8
2000	133.1	306.3	151.5	36.9	41.1	402.9	1,071.8
2001	187.9	361.9	185.1	42.7	60.2	443.4	1,281.2
2002	221.7	397.9	286.5	44.5	74.4	518.2	1,543.2
2003	234.5	401.9	346.0	44.3	99.2	567.8	1,693.7
2004	232.1	390.7	454.0	42.2	115.2	593.6	1,827.8
2005	219.7	356.7	551.1	34.5	153.2	640.0	1,955.2
2006	202.4	339.9	581.2	28.8	183.6	794.5	2,130.4
2007	198.5	347.8	585.6	26.9	243.9	1,069.7	2,472.4
2008	137.7	314.1	395.5	20.0	239.5	1565.0	2,671.8

Source: Gary Gorton, *Slapped in the Face by the Invisible Hand: Banking and the Panic of 2007* 26 (May 9, 2009), http://www.frbatlanta.org/news/CONFEREN /09fmc/gor ton.pdf (citing Bond Market Association, Bloomberg).

How do shadow banks work? In order to serve a similar function as conventional banks, shadow banks need to create an asset that is perceived by the public as "just as good" as a bank deposit. This in turn means creating an asset that is "informationallyinsensitive," meaning that the holder does not need to do material due diligence, but can just take it on faith that the asset can be turned into cash at par on demand. Many different examples of the shadow banking system have developed over the past several decades, including structured investment vehicles (SIVs), investment banks like Bear Stearns and Lehman Brothers, and finance companies like CIT.

The shadow banking system essentially dis-intermediated many of the activities of the conventional banking system: deposits became un-insured money market instruments and loans became securitizations. And like the conventional banking system prior to the establishment of the FDIC and the Fed, the shadow banking system was inherently vulnerable to runs if its liabilities were to become "informationally *sensitive*" – that is, if the holders of the shadow banking system's short-dated liabilities concluded they could no longer take it on faith that they could get their money back on demand at par, a run could ensue.

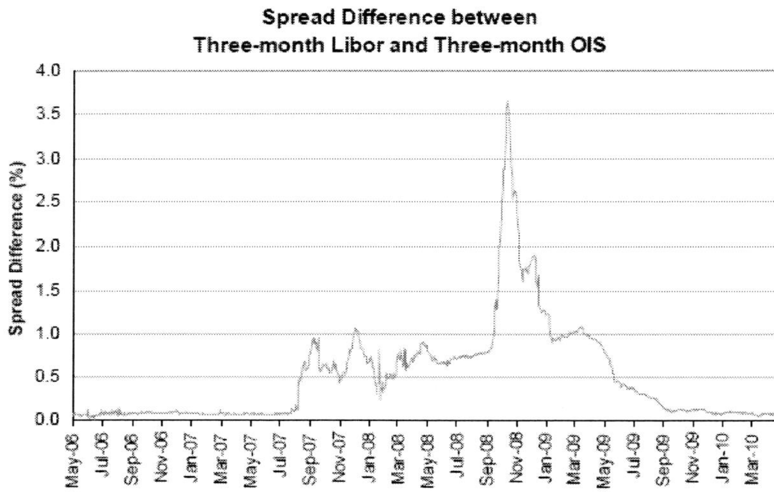

Source: Bloomberg.

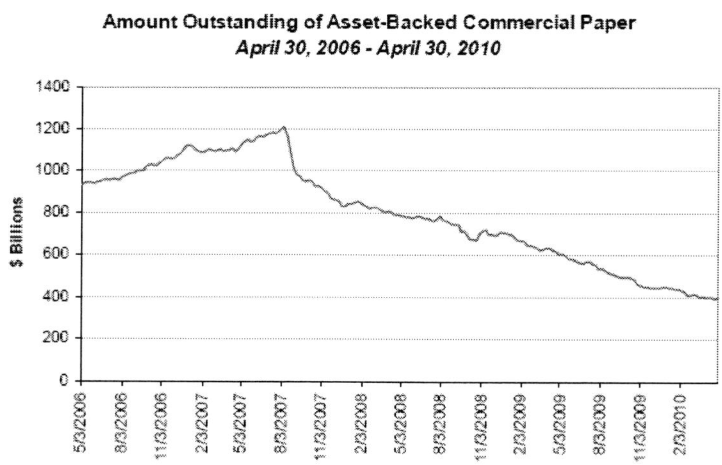

Source: Federal Reserve.

And indeed, a run on the shadow banking system was one of the defining characteristics of the most recent financial crisis. A pivotal moment was August 9, 2007, when Bank Paribas (BNP) said that it could not value the toxic mortgage assets in three of its off-balance sheet vehicles, and that, therefore, the liability holders, who thought they could get out at any time, were frozen.[3] This began the liquidity crisis in the shadow banking system, as the investing public rightly concluded that even the most senior, short-dated liabilities of the system had become "informationally-sensitive." The following charts show the breakdown in unsecured interbank lending, as reflected by the extraordinary widening in LIBOR spreads, and the precipitous fall in the volume of outstanding Asset Backed Commercial Paper that were triggered by the events of August 9th.

THE CRISIS OF THE SYSTEM

The crisis *within* the shadow banking system did not become disorderly and paralyzing to the financial system until September 15, 2008, the day that it became a crisis *of* the shadow banking system. That day, of course, was when Lehman Brothers failed. So why was one aspect of the crisis apparently containable and orderly, and another uncontrollable and disorderly? The answer has to do with legal authority.

In March 2008, the Federal Reserve evoked Section 13-3 of the Federal Reserve Act[4] in order to make a loan that facilitated the merger of Bear Stearns, which was under a vicious run, into JPMorgan. Concurrently, the Fed opened its balance sheet to the investment banks that were primary dealers, including, most importantly, the institutions that were referred to as "the big four." The program under which this was carried out was called the Primary Dealer Credit Facility.[5]

Markets calmed for a time. But when Lehman experienced a similar run to that which engulfed Bear Stearns, the Federal Reserve could not facilitate a Bear-like rescue, because, according to Fed Chairman Bernanke, Lehman lacked adequate collateral which therefore constrained the Fed's legal authority to intervene.[6] In the wake of Lehman's failure, the on-going run on the shadow banking system morphed into an intensely disorderly process, which was further exacerbated by the Reserve Primary Money Market Fund "breaking the buck,"[7] owing to its holdings of Lehman commercial paper.

Extraordinary actions by our government, and governments around the world, were required to stop the liquidity crisis. What the government had to do was to provide the shadow banking system with similar safety nets as the conventional banking system. And the Federal Reserve, the FDIC and the Treasury did essentially that.

The Federal Reserve created a host of special lending facilities, serving as a liquidity provider of last resort to the entire financial system, including money market funds holding Asset Backed Commercial Paper. The FDIC increased deposit insurance limits, totally uncapping them on transaction accounts, while creating its Temporary Liquidity Guarantee Program,[8] which allowed financial institutions – conventional banks and shadow banks as well – to issue, for a fee, unsecured debt with the full faith and credit of the United States.

The Treasury Department created an insurance program for money market funds,[9] mirroring the FDIC's insurance for bank deposits. And, of course, the Treasury Department ultimately, after the passage of TARP, provided equity capital to financial institutions, both conventional banks and former shadow banks that had converted to bank holding companies.[10]

None of us can know the counterfactual, and ultimately historians will provide the final assessment of the actions taken by our government. But as we sit here today in the immediate post-crisis period, it is reasonable to assert that the response by the government was in fact absolutely necessary.

Had the run on the shadow banking system not been arrested, the consequences for our economy would have certainly been much more severe, potentially catastrophic.

CONCLUSION

There are many conclusions to be drawn from the financial crisis. One of them is that our public officials responded boldly during a period of tremendous uncertainty and peril.

And our nation owes them our gratitude. For me, the most important lesson is that the shadow banking system is indeed a banking system, engaged in the same type of activity as conventional banks: maturity, liquidity and credit quality transformation.

Because the shadow banking system lacks the regulatory framework and FDIC and Federal Reserve backstops that the conventional banking system enjoys, its inherent vulnerability to runs persists.

Going forward, the realities of the shadow banking system should be understood and reform enacted accordingly. A key guidepost for reform of our financial regulatory structure is simple: what an institution does, not what it is called, should determine how it is regulated.

Mr. Chairman, Mr. Vice-Chairman, and honorable members of the Commission, I would like to thank you once again for the opportunity to appear before you today and for your work on behalf of our country.

I look forward to your questions.

End Notes

[1] Paul McCulley, The Shadow Banking System and Hyman Minsky's Economic Journey, *PIMCO* (May 2009), http://media.pimco-global.com/pdfs/pdf/GCB%20Focus%20May%2009.pdf?WT.cg_n=PIMCOUS&WT.ti=GCB%20Focus%20May%2009.pdf.

[2] Paul McCulley, The Shadow Banking System and Hyman Minsky's Economic Journey, *PIMCO* 2 (May 2009), http://media. ("Since shadow banks don't have access to the same governmental safety nets that real banks have, they don't have to operate under meaningful regulatory constraints, notably for the amount of leverage they can use, the size of their liquidity buffers and the type of lending and investing they can do. To be sure, shadow banking needed some seal of approval, so that providers of short-dated funding could convince themselves that their claims were de facto "just as good" as deposits at banks with access to the government's liquidity safety nets. Conveniently, the friendly faces at the rating agencies, paid by the shadow bankers, stood at the ready to provide such seals of approval. Moody's and S&P would put an A-1/P-1 rating on the commercial paper, which in turn would be bought by money market funds. Of course, it's inherently an unstable structure. The rating agencies face an in-built problem of putting ratings on new innovations, because they haven't had a chance to observe a historical track record – to see their performance over a full cycle.").

[3] Sebastian Boyd, BNP Paribas Freezes Funds as Loan Losses Roil Markets, *Bloomberg*, Aug. 9, 2007, http://www.bloomberg.com/apps/news?pid=20601087&refer =home&sid=aNIJ.UO9 Pzxw (last visited May 3, 3010) ("BNP Paribas SA, France's biggest bank, halted withdrawals from three investment funds because it couldn't 'fairly' value their holdings after U.S. subprime mortgage losses roiled credit markets.").

[4] That section provides: In unusual and exigent circumstances, the Board of Governors of the Federal Reserve System, by the affirmative vote of not less than five members, may authorize any Federal reserve bank, during such periods as the said board may determine, at rates established in accordance with the provisions of section 357 of this title, to discount for any individual, partnership, or corporation, notes, drafts, and bills of exchange when such notes, drafts, and bills of exchange are indorsed or otherwise secured to the satisfaction of the Federal reserve bank: *Provided*, That before discounting any such note, draft, or bill of exchange for an individual or a partnership or corporation the Federal reserve bank shall obtain evidence that such individual, partnership, or corporation is unable to secure adequate credit accommodations from other banking institutions. All such discounts for individuals, partnerships, or corporations shall be subject to such limitations, restrictions, and regulations as the Board of Governors of the Federal Reserve System may prescribe. Federal Reserve Act § 13-3, 12 U.S.C. § 343 (2006).

[5] Primary Dealer Credit Facility: Frequently Asked Questions, *Federal Reserve Bank of New York*, http://www.newyorkfed.org/markets/pdcf_faq.html (last visited May 3, 2010) ("The Primary Dealer Credit Facility (PDCF) is an overnight loan facility that will provide funding to primary dealers in exchange for any tri-party-eligible collateral and is intended to foster the functioning of financial markets more generally.").

[6] Ben S. Bernanke, Chairman, Bd. of Governors of the Fed. Reserve Sys., Public Policy Issues Raised by the Report of the Lehman Bankruptcy Examiner, Testimony Before the House Committee on Financial Services (Apr. 20, 2010) (transcript available at http://www.house.gov/apps/list/hearing/financialsvcs_dem/ bernanke_4.20.10.pdf) ("The Federal Reserve fully understood that the failure of Lehman would shake the financial system and the economy. However, the only tool available to the Federal Reserve to address

the situation was its ability to provide short-term liquidity against adequate collateral; and, as I noted, Lehman already had access to our emergency credit facilities. It was clear, though, that Lehman needed both substantial capital and an open-ended guarantee of its obligations to open for business on Monday, September 15. At that time, neither the Federal Reserve nor any other agency had the authority to provide capital or an unsecured guarantee, and thus no means of preventing Lehman's failure existed.").

[7] John Waggoner, Reserve Primary Money Market Fund Breaks a Buck, *USAToday.com*, Sept. 16, 2008, http://www.usatoday.com/money/perfi/basics/2008-09-16-damage_N.htm ("If you want to know how severe the financial industry crisis is, here's further proof: The share price of the Reserve Primary fund, a money market mutual fund, has fallen below the sacred $1 mark, thanks to the Lehman Bros. meltdown.").

[8] Temporary Liquidity Guarantee Program Frequently Asked Questions, *Federal Deposit Insurance Corporation*, http://www.fdic.gov/regulations (last visited May 3, 2010) ("On October 20, 2009, the FDIC established a limited, six-month emergency guarantee facility upon expiration of the Debt Guarantee Program. Under this emergency guarantee facility, certain participating entities can apply to the FDIC for permission to issue FDIC-guaranteed debt during the period starting October 31, 2009 through April 30, 2010. The fee for issuing debt under the emergency facility will be at least 300 basis points, which the FDIC reserves the right to increase on a case-by-case basis, depending upon the risks presented by the issuing entity.").

[9] Treasury Announces Guarantee Program for Money Market Funds, *Press Room U.S. Department of the Treasury*, http://www.ustreas.gov/press/releases/hp1147.htm (last visited May 3, 2010) ("The U.S. Treasury Department today announced the establishment of a temporary guaranty program for the U.S. money market mutual fund industry. For the next year, the U.S. Treasury will insure the holdings of any publicly offered eligible money market mutual fund – both retail and institutional – that pays a fee to participate in the program.").

[10] Treasury Announces TARP Capital Purchase Program Description, *Press Room U.S. Department of the Treasury*, http://www.ustreas.gov/press/releases/hp1207.htm (last visited May 3, 2010) ("Treasury today announced a voluntary Capital Purchase Program to encourage U.S. financial institutions to build capital to increase the flow of financing to U.S. businesses and consumers and to support the U.S. economy.").

In: Shadow Banking and Its Role ... ISBN: 978-1- 62081-703-2
Editors: D. A. Jenkins and M. I. Collins

Chapter 5

COMMENTS ON "REGULATING THE SHADOW BANKING SYSTEM" BY DANIEL K. TARULLO, MEMBER, BOARD OF GOVERNORS OF THE FEDERAL RESERVE SYSTEM*

Broadly speaking, threats to financial stability can arise in two ways: first, through the rapid deterioration or failure of a large institution with leverage sufficient to have widespread knock-on effects and, second, through the breakdown of a significant market in which large numbers of leveraged actors depend upon similar sources of liquidity and, importantly, backup liquidity in periods of stress. These two sources of systemic risk can be, and usually are, related. In fact, the severity of the recent crisis might be explained as an explosive combination of the two. But the different origins of risk call for different or, perhaps more precisely, complementary, policy responses.[1]

To date, reform in financial regulation and supervision has focused mainly on large regulated institutions: Three examples are the just-announced Basel III capital rules, much of the Dodd-Frank Act, and the Federal Reserve's revamping of its large holding company supervision. Of course, attention has also been paid to the second source of systemic risk, notably in DoddFrank's provisions for prudential supervision of payments, clearing, and settlement systems. But more will need to be done in this area, particularly as new

* This is an edited, reformatted and augmented version of comments given on September 17, 2010, before the Brookings Panel on Economic Activity.

constraints applicable to large regulated institutions push more activity into the unregulated sector.

The paper by Gary Gorton and Andrew Metrick, "Regulating the Shadow Banking System" (G-M), fits squarely within this enterprise. It builds on two important insights from work Gorton had pursued well before the financial crisis began: First, that the enormous growth of the shadow banking system generally, and the repurchase agreement, or "repo," market specifically, depended on the engineering of AAA-rated securities that led participants to believe they did not need to inquire into the soundness of the underlying collateral. This financial engineering largely succeeded in insulating participants from idiosyncratic risk. But when the value of whole classes of the underlying collateral was drawn into serious question, initially by the collapse of the subprime housing market, participants' lack of information about the collateral they held led to a shattering of confidence in all the collateral.

In the absence of the regulation and government backstop that have applied to the traditional banking system since the Depression, a run on assets in the entire repo market ensued. The resulting forced sale of assets into an illiquid market turned many illiquid institutions into insolvent ones. The fallout has been such that, to this day, the amount of repo funding available for non-agency, mortgage-backed securities, commercial mortgage-backed securities, high-yield corporate bonds, and other instruments backed by assets with any degree of risk remains substantially below its pre-Lehman levels.

The second Gorton insight on which the paper builds is the importance of statutory franchise value for the business model viability of at least some kinds of regulated financial entities. Where competition from unregulated entities is permitted, explicitly or de facto, capital and other requirements imposed on regulated firms may shrink margins enough to make them unattractive to investors. The result, as we have seen in the past, will be some combination of regulatory arbitrage, assumption of higher risk in permitted activities, and exit from the industry. Each of these outcomes at least potentially undermines the original motivation for the regulation.

The G-M paper provides a concrete, though in some respects not fully elaborated, proposal to remedy the information problem in the repo market through creation of statutory franchise value for what G-M calls Narrow Funding Banks (NFBs). These banks would be "narrow" in that their only assets would be asset-backed securities (ABS) and very high quality instruments such as Treasuries. They would, it appears, make their money from the income streams associated with the ABS. They would raise the funds to purchase ABS through debt issuance and, most significantly for the proposal, the repo market, in which the collateral offered would be liabilities of the NFBs. The government would regulate the NFBs directly, as it does all banks, but also by setting requirements for the ABS that could be bought by the NFBs. This regulation is intended to provide market confidence in the liabilities of the NFBs, which would be further buttressed by NFB access to the discount window.

A key feature of the proposal is that, by law, *only* NFBs could buy securitized assets. The consequent franchise value would compensate NFBs for the costs they incur because they can hold only high-quality securities, are subject to supervision and prudential requirements, and have to operate in a highly transparent fashion. In essence, ABS-backed repo funding would be limited to NFBs.

The first two questions I would pose about this creative policy proposal are the most basic: What problem is it supposed to solve, and how does the breadth of the remedy align with that problem? Given their analysis of the breakdown of the repo market, Gorton and Metrick's answer might be self-evident: The G-M proposal aims to solve the information problems that increased the risk from maturity transformation associated with ABS repo funding. This, of course, is not solving for the entire shadow banking system, though an effective plan for reforming the ABS repo market would be a major accomplishment in itself.[2]

But in proposing a solution to this problem, G-M would significantly restrict *all* asset-backed securitization. While it is obvious that too much credit was created through ABS and associated instruments in the years preceding the crisis, it seems at least reasonable to question whether the best policy response is this dramatic a change in the regulatory environment. One wonders, for example, if it is desirable to forbid anyone but NFBs from buying ABS, particularly if there are investors interested in holding these assets regardless of their utility in repo arrangements. The severe problems now associated with ABS began with assets held by mismatched entities like structured investment vehicles or financial institutions engaged in capital arbitrage under Basel II, not those held by end investors.

A variant on this initial question is how much the legal environment for securitization should be changed in order to provide a source of stable short-term liquidity in wholesale funding markets. Limiting securitization purchases to NFBs will surely result in some tailoring of ABS to the business models of NFBs, an outcome that might not be identical to a securitization market tailored to the funding needs of lenders providing credit to businesses and consumers. Also, as I will explain later, the G-M proposal would require non-trivial changes in bank regulatory policy, as well as the significant extension of discount window access to a new kind of institution. All this would be in pursuit of a mechanism for generating large amounts of liquidity. A cost-benefit discussion is probably needed at the outset, with careful specification of the benefits of the repo market that G-M are trying to save, weighed against the likely impact on--among other things--the securitization market and regulatory system.

A second set of questions concerns how the NFBs would operate in practice. As a threshold matter, it is worth noting that policymakers may find the proposal to have a certain binary quality. That is, it would structurally change the entire securitization market and a large portion of the repo market essentially overnight. In effect, G-M put all securitization eggs into one basket. If the new system worked well, the benefits presumably would be significant, and perhaps quickly realized. Indeed, the new system might succeed in helping to restart, on a sounder basis, various ABS submarkets that remain largely dormant three years after the crisis began to unfold.[3] If, on the other hand, the new system encountered major difficulties, there might be materially reduced adaptive capacity in other financial actors, possibly for a considerable period.

One obvious source of difficulty is the possibility, well recognized by G-M, that the business model mandated for NFBs might not be viable and stable. As with all forms of narrow banks proposed over the years, NFBs as a group would seem likely to generate relatively low revenues, given the low risk of the securities in which they would have to invest. G-M propose to counter this problem by granting franchise value through the statutory monopoly on securitization mentioned earlier and through access to the Federal Reserve's discount window. Picking up on their analogy to the creation of deposit insurance in the 1930s, the monopoly on securitization is intended to help offset the regulatory costs imposed on NFBs in the same way that the monopoly on the "business of banking" was intended to offset the regulatory costs imposed on insured depository institutions.

Unlike the business environment for banks in the 1930s, however, securitization and repo lending are national--if not international--activities, with little to suggest that any advantage would be derived from local knowledge. It seems quite possible that the economies of scale associated with the NFB model are sufficiently high that the industry structure would tend toward oligopoly, or even monopoly. That is, too *much* franchise value might be created. In that event, there would be significant additions to the cost side of the proposal's ledger, in the form of the price and quantity effects that result from non-competitive industry structures. Regardless of the eventual structure of the industry, NFBs essentially would be monolines, with highly correlated risk exposures. They could be particularly vulnerable to funding difficulties in times of deteriorating credit conditions. Yet by the terms of the G-M proposal, they apparently would not be able to hedge interest rate or other risks. G-M propose giving NFBs access to the discount window to forestall liquidity problems and runs on the NFBs, presumably in the same way that deposit insurance stopped runs on traditional banks. Here again though, the analogy is not a perfect one. While banks and their depositors are assured that the Federal Deposit Insurance Corporation will keep the latter whole in the event of the former's failure, the Federal Reserve does not make binding commitments to lend to any institution and actively discourages reliance on the window for regular funding.

A third question about the G-M proposal arises because of the significant changes in current law and practice that would be required were the proposal to be adopted. The prohibition on ABS holdings by anyone other than NFBs is the obvious and major example. But there are several others: In addition to the possibly problematic features of discount window lending in general for the proposal, the Federal Reserve has traditionally opened the window to non-depository institutions only in particularly stressed conditions. Under the Dodd-Frank Act, any use of credit ratings in federal regulations will be prohibited, an obvious complication to the GM proposal. This part of Dodd-Frank has accelerated and expanded the efforts already underway at the federal banking agencies to lessen regulatory reliance on ratings. In truth, it may pose no greater challenge for the G-M proposal than for many existing capital rules.[4] Still, it may require extension of G-M's confidence that the regulator could adequately oversee ABS ratings to confidence that it could assign ratings in the first place. I would observe that the substantial effort expended by staff at the Board and the Federal Reserve Bank of New York to evaluate the creditworthiness of a relatively small number of securitizations in the Term Asset-Backed Securities Loan Facility suggests the enormity of that task. Furthermore, the wisdom of having a government agency--even the independent central bank--assume such a permanent, central role in credit allocation should at least be subject to debate.

A final regulatory issue is raised by another G-M response to their expectation that equity returns for NFBs will be lower than for traditional banks. In place of the equity capital requirements generally applicable to banking organizations, G-M propose that NFBs would issue capital notes that are debt-like except in periods of stress, when they would convert to equity. In essence, all of an NFB's capital would be contingent capital. While contingent capital is an item on the financial regulatory agenda, it is considered a possible supplement to common equity, not a substitute for it. In this respect, the G-M proposal moves in the opposite direction from Basel III, which has followed markets in making common equity the centerpiece of capital evaluation and requirements.[5]

These inconsistencies with current law and practice in the G-M proposal do not themselves argue against its soundness. They do, however, underscore the degree to which the NFBs would require development of a new financial regulatory approach, as well as a restructuring of the ABS and repo markets.

More generally, the existence of costs or problems does not counsel the rejection of the proposal as such. In the face of very real flaws in the pre-crisis state of these markets, and the failure of some ABS markets to recover, even where it seems they could function sensibly, there is a very good case for a policy initiative. So let me consider briefly whether variants on the basic G-M approach might retain its core benefits while addressing some of its potential problems. One possibility would be to broaden the permissible ownership of NFBs to include bank holding companies. This modification would make the most sense if one believed that the basic G-M approach was promising but that the risks of either an untenable business model or high industry concentration, and consequent anti-competitive effects, were high. It is possible that a number of large, diversified financial holding companies would find an NFB a viable part of their operations. G-M require that NFBs be stand-alone entities, and specifically prohibit ownership by commercial banks in an effort to avoid implicit contractual guarantees. This is a legitimate concern, to be sure, but one that might be at least imperfectly addressed through specific restrictions on relationships between affiliates in a bank holding company. The relevant comparison is thus between the residual costs of the regulated relationship and the effects of an anti-competitive industry structure.

A second variant on the G-M approach, also motivated by industry structure problems, would be to turn NFBs from privately owned public utilities (as G-M describe them) to actual public utilities. However, the extent to which this change in ownership structure would ameliorate the anti-competitive problems is uncertain. Moreover, the concerns mentioned earlier with respect to government judgments on credit allocation would remain, even if they are provided another layer of insulation through the device of a government corporation. In addition, of course, the history of Fannie Mae and Freddie Mac is a cautionary tale of the potential for a government monopoly with a conservative mandate to expand its operation into much riskier activities.

At first glance, then, it is not at all clear that structural modifications to the basic G-M approach would be preferable to the proposal as they have described it. Options that depart from the G-M approach would need to find different ways of solving the information problems that G-M identify. Let me briefly speculate about possible alternatives that would use regulatory requirements to create a class of ABS in which markets could, without inquiry into the nature and quality of the underlying assets, have confidence even in periods of stress. One way, of course, would be to follow more closely the deposit insurance analogy by establishing an insurance system. G-M suggest that an insurance system for the repo market would be impractical, question whether insuring collateral (i.e., certain classes of securitized assets) would be sustainable without creating franchise value, and worry that the creation of franchise value through limiting entry into securitization would, in their words, "limit the amount of money created." Yet, as I suggested earlier, the G-M proposal itself might constrain securitization in undesirable ways, both related and unrelated to repo transactions. In addressing the franchise value issue, it would be interesting to pursue an important idea that G-M mention, but which is not at the center of their proposal: making the repo bankruptcy exception available only where the collateral conforms to certain criteria established by law or regulation. Given the demand for repo funding, it seems worth considering whether this device could be used to create the necessary franchise value. Indeed, if this approach had promise, it might be feasible for a regulatory body to establish the requisite criteria without providing insurance. With or without insurance, the "franchise value" might attach more to the instrument than to an institution.

There is not time here to enumerate the potential difficulties with these ideas, but they are not hard to discern, even as stated in such skeletal form. In common with the G-M proposal, they would require a level of expertise and involvement in credit rating by the government that could pose practical and, in some conceivable alternatives, policy concerns. In any case, these are thoughts for further discussion, rather than developed options. Gary Gorton and Andrew Metrick have, in setting forth this proposal, continued to shape our understanding of the role and risks of the shadow banking system, as well as to add a specific proposal to our menu of possible responses.

End Notes

[1] The views presented here are my own and not necessarily those of other members of the Board of Governors of the Federal Reserve System or the Federal Open Market Committee. Tom King and Michael Palumbo of the Board staff contributed to these remarks.

[2] For a survey of the entire shadow banking system, see Pozsar, Zoltan, Tobian Adrian, Adam Ashcraft, and Hayley Boesky (July 2010): "Shadow Banking," *Federal Reserve Bank of New York Staff Reports*, no. 458. (The report is available at www.newyorkfed.org /research/staff_reports/sr458.pdf.)

[3] The relative dormancy of these markets is also due in part to the limited supply of the loans needed to feed the securitization process.

[4] For a discussion of some of the issues raised in the context of capital requirements, see Board of Governors of the Federal Reserve System (2010), "Advance Notice of Proposed Rulemaking Regarding Alternatives to the Use of Credit Ratings in the Risk-Based Capital Guidelines of the Federal Banking Agencies," Joint Advance Notice of Proposed Rulemaking (August 10), www.federalreserve.gov/newsevents/press/bcreg/bcreg 20100810 a1.pdf.

[5] It also seems likely that the kinds of quantitative liquidity requirements currently under development by the Basel Committee on Banking Supervision would be difficult for NFBs to satisfy.

INDEX

F

G

M

O

P

R

S

T